W9-BBC-255

THE REVOLUTIONARY IDEA
IN FRANCE

1789-1871

BY

LORD ELTON

FELLOW OF QUEEN'S COLLEGE, OXFORD

NEW YORK

Howard Fertig

1969

First published in 1923; 2nd edition 1931 [here reprinted]

HOWARD FERTIG, INC. EDITION 1969
Published by arrangement with Edward Arnold & Co.

Library of Congress Catalog Card Number: 68-9657

PRINTED IN THE UNITED STATES OF AMERICA
BY NOBLE OFFSET PRINTERS, INC.

FOREWORD TO THE FIRST EDITION

I SHOULD like to make clear what I have tried to do in
this little book. There are plenty of histories of the first
French Revolution of (roughly) 1789-1830, and one or
two of the second of (roughly) 1830-1871, and this, I
need hardly say, is not one of them. On the contrary,
it is an attempt to present very briefly and to make
intelligible what essentially, beneath all the distracting
complexity of events, these great movements of the
human spirit in France were attempting to do, and what,
beneath all their distracting complexities, they actually
accomplished.

The average student of the history of these tre-
mendously important years can usually spare them only
a limited number of hours, and although he can usually
amass a respectable knowledge of their principal events
he very often fails altogether to achieve anything like
an intellectual grasp of their meaning as a whole ; he
cannot get at the heart of them. I have done what I can
here to present the essence of the great problem for his
benefit. Naturally in so doing, I have sometimes come
near writing, incidentally, a skeleton outline of the
political history of the time : and in this, I think, there
is another advantage. For too many histories of the
Revolution clearly understand, and encourage their
readers to understand, by " the Revolution " nothing

less than the complete history of France from 1789 to 1830 (or rather to 1799, where they have usually for convenience sake, but quite unphilosophically, to break off the narrative.)

Now apart from the confusion which, as I have just suggested, this too often causes to the reader, it has another, and an even greater, defect. For if this is the meaning of " the Revolution " the Revolution becomes— if I may quote what I have written in the course of the following pages—not only all the cruel and extravagant measures, but actually all the counter-revolutionary measures, of those years. The French Revolution is *la Vendée* and the *émigrés* as well as the *noyades* and the Place de la Guillotine. It is, in a word, both Marat and Charlotte Corday. And consequently it becomes fatally easy for historian or student, selecting, whether maliciously or at random, from the vast complexity of its records to misrepresent the Revolution as sanguinary, meaningless and incoherent. In truth, I submit, the Revolution is *not* all the recorded events of the years over which it extended, *but*—the French people's deep and instinctive sense of the need of certain changes, and their efforts, beneath certain easily distinguishable distractions, to accomplish them.

I have tried to disengage and present this effort, and the theories it followed or implied, in successive phases, each a problem in itself and all together containing (were any human being able to see to the bottom of them all) the meaning and explanation of the whole Revolution.

Naturally I have omitted lavishly. Most surprising of these omissions it may seem that I have said so little of the religious problem in the Revolution. This is not because I think it unimportant. In itself it is of extreme importance, but in my opinion (there are authorities for the contrary) the conflict with the Church is not essential to the understanding of the Revolution. Without it there might have been no *Vendée*, the king might have been less quickly and completely alienated, but the Revolution would have followed its central course unchanged.

I might have brought this brief study to an end in 1830, for in that year the first Revolution, triumphant over the determined attempt under the Bourbon Restoration to resurrect the *ancien régime en bloc*, becomes finally an established and conservative force— save only for that small aggressive residue embodied in the movement for its logical completion in the Republic. But the revolutionary movement which about 1830 begins to take shape in a new revolutionary idea not only lies so close to the roots of the most urgent problem of our own day but reproduces so many features of the first that the two deserve unmistakably not to be separated, and each must gain from the juxtaposition. For indeed the deepest waters of the revolutionary idea flow alike beneath the surface currents of both its aspects : the belief, I mean, in the possibilities of Revolution as a method.

The revolutionary idea, as it works itself out in its twofold form through the history of France from 1789 to 1871 (for the histories which break off their narrative in 1799 or in 1814 can never present more than a part of the truth) is of interest not only to the special student. It is a golden mine of precept and warning for all observers of politics to-day, the richest of all mines for quarrying. It is the key not only to modern France but to modern Europe. I hope that at a time when there is so much talk, and so little thinking, about revolutions, this little study may be of some service to the general reader. In all countries politicians discuss Revolution, but only in the history of France can Revolution be scientifically studied.

If this little sketch is useful it will have fulfilled its object. It has been written in three different countries, and sometimes out of reach of libraries. I hope that some of its shortcomings may be charitably ascribed to that fact. I only wish they all could.

FOREWORD TO THE SECOND EDITION

I HAVE used the occasion of the issue of a second and cheaper edition of this short study of Revolution to make some minor corrections, mainly typographical. Otherwise it remains unaltered.

CONTENTS

CHAPTER I

THE OUTBREAK

WHEN did the French Revolution begin ? There is no answer to that question. Precise dates, picturesque " outbreaks," these are the conventions and conveniences of history ; and Revolution is a process too subtle for such methods. It is inevitable no doubt that for every-day purposes one should speak of the " outbreak " of the continuous Revolution and hit upon such a date as May 5th, the first sitting of the States-General, or (worse) July 14th, the taking of the Bastille. The fact remains that the Revolution was in being many years before May 5th ; nor was any new principle to come suddenly into the world that day. It is true that in their first exhilaration (as we shall see) the men of 1789 did their best to break completely with the past, " to cut their destiny in two," honestly believing that in their hands the great age was to begin again. But the past, as always, was stronger than they.

De Tocqueville's *Ancien Régime* showed, more than fifty years ago, that in the ten years after 1789 the Revolutionaries did in fact build the new of the débris of the old. And naturally even that seemed to the men of his day a paradox, brought up, as they had been, to think of 1789 as a complete cleavage with tradition. But we can go further perhaps than de Tocqueville. We shall not see merely an abrupt catastrophe, followed by a gradual revival of much that had seemed destroyed. Rather, we may agree, at no time was there a bridgeless gulf between old and new. The fine illusions of " the men of 1789," " the Idealogues," it is true, persuaded France for a little while to believe that the tremendous past was soon to be no more than a small cloud drifting far away. And so, as we shall see, between 1789 and 1792 the true Revolution is cut across by this artificial Idealogue effort to escape from the bonds of tradition. And we shall find that what was to endure of the achievements of the Revolution, that small essential part of them which was *real*, was, broadly speaking, not to be effected before 1792. But for the moment all that concerns us is to realise that 1789 may be more truly thought of as the continuation of a gradual process, than (as was universally supposed at the time) as the catastrophic revelation of forces and principles altogether unprecedented.

It was only long examination of the particulars of evidence that persuaded de Tocqueville of the paradox, as it seemed to him, that the same forms and processes were to be discovered on either side of the explosion. To-day psychology alone, and *a priori*, before we had approached the evidence, would predispose us to expect these conclusions. For whatever psychology has, or has not, established, it is certain that the thoughts and actions of men are in a great measure determined by their thoughts and actions in the past. If the fathers have eaten sour grapes not only will the teeth of the children be set on edge, but the odds are that they will continue to eat sour grapes. A nation, like a man, is the creature of its past. And so we shall be forewarned against the noble delusion of the Idealogues of 1789, of Condorcet, who thought that " the world might be emancipated by burning its records." At most we shall expect to find in 1789 the liberation of forces hitherto repressed.

We have been too long hypnotised by the word Revolution, by the memory of old bloodshed, too ready to assume that Revolution is the anti-thesis of Evolution. But after all, even the most South American of revolutions demands some preparation, fixes some roots in the past. And from the South American Revolution upwards to what we call solemnly the evolutionary process, it is but a question of degree. I am inclined to believe that the more deeply this, or any other, Revolution is studied the further its roots will be found reaching into the past, the less possible will it seem to select a particular date for its origination. Only, at some stage in the gradual process will have intruded some picturesque and resonant event, an oath in a tennis-court, the flight of a king, a massacre, to embitter, or deafen, or mislead : and the historian, keen scented always for the event, will have made it so overshadowing in his picture that we shall be easily enough persuaded that something altogether different in kind has superseded the less adventurous evolution we had been content to trace. But, when we see clearly, it is not so.

Let us expect, then, to find the central process of the years that followed 1789 anticipated in the dimmer light of the *ancien régime*.

What, broadly, then, is the process for which we are to look, this essential achievement of the years 1789 to 1792 ? Broadly, and very briefly, it we may look this much ahead, we may say that in these years the middle class became a privileged oligarchy in place of the hitherto privileged, the feudal aristocracy. And the blind driving power behind it, what insured the

acquiescence of the court (which would never have surrendered to the respectabilities of the States-General
alone), was an apparently accidental upheaval of the
poor, the nameless miserables who took the Bastille,
and brought the royal family through the October
twilight to Paris from Versailles. In spite of which the
new oligarchs neglected as completely as they were
able the distresses of those to whom they owed their
triumph. Save for the very partial abolition of feudalism
on August 4th, 1789, into which it had been frightened
by the peasants themselves, the Constituent Assembly
ignored the majority of the nation. The gulf between
the Declaration of Rights and the Constitution of 1791,
the retention of so much of the feudal system whose
demise was trumpeted on August 4th, these were the
measure of their treachery to those nameless ones.
The middle class first neglecting and then using the
miseries of the politically unconscious masses for the
purposes of their own deliberate assault upon power
and privilege—let us keep an eye open then for the
counterpart of this process as we explore the further
side of that July of 1789.

An accepted commonplace distinguishes the political
from the social Revolution, but in fact all revolutions
are social revolutions. For *pace* Aristotle, man is very
much more a social than a political animal and is only
incited to the effort and danger of Revolution-making
(as to other forms of effort and danger) by discomforts
which reach out and touch him where he sits by his own
fireside. But at the end of the 18th century more than
ever before or since men believed that social evils could
be healed by political formulæ. And so the literature
and the records of this time are littered with the jargon

of " Contracts " and " Constitutions." These men did really suppose that some mysterious lost contract between king and people, some constitution yet unframed, would be miraculously the end of all their personal disquietudes. But for our present purpose such talk is but the symptom of the disease. And the disease, which we are to diagnose, was social.

What then were the principal discontents of the French people in 1789 ? And first what were the particular grievances of that middle class whose assault on the privilege of the class above it and neglect of the distress of the class below it occupied the beginning of the Revolution ?

France was bankrupt ; a fact of tremendous importance. The despotism which governed her was a disorganised despotism. Communications, administration, above everything finances—all were in a state of chaos. Above all, finances. No government contract was even a reasonably safe speculation ; the contractor might always be unable to recover from the government his expenses upon ship-building or road-making or the provisioning of troops ; investors could never be certain that their interest would be paid. The wealth and enterprise of the middle classes had been growing fast through the last decades of the old order ; they were consumed already with the eternal craving of the *rentier*, great or small, for a safe investment. *There were no safe investments under the ancien régime.* The French Revolution, like its States-General, began as a financial counsel of despair. The States-General—it is essential to remember —was convoked because there was no other means left of raising money for the Treasury. The system of taxation had to be revised. Unfortunately in a feudal society to readjust taxation was to re-adjust—society. But that

was not clearly realised by those who summoned the
States-General. They thought of their experiment as
a fiscal, not a political, expedient. Even Mirabeau
considered that the entire business might have been
disposed of in a week, so widely was concern concentrated
upon the merely fiscal disorder.

Necker was the hero of the moment, the delight of
the nation. All France trusted him—passionately.
Why ? Because he was a successful banker. He had
managed the Thelusson-Necker bank admirably : surely
then this was the man to save bankrupt France ? But it
was not only bankruptcy that France needed to be saved
from. Or rather her bankruptcy was a symptom, not
the malady itself. But it was natural that the middle
classes should think first, when reform was in the air,
of financial reform. The increased activity and enterprise of the State during the last twenty years had
brought it into direct financial relation with a growing
number of its citizens ; the fortunes of these men were
bound up with those of the government ; if not salaried
by it they had lent it money, speculated in its markets,
contracted for its public works. And so the incompetence
and dishonesty of its financial administration was not
merely a public or political question : it was becoming
a spectre which sat by a thousand hearths. From
somewhere before the middle of the 18th century in
France must date that twofold passion for prosperity
and for safety which has come to be thought of as typical
of the middle classes. But whereas normally this passion
makes of the middle classes the most conservative force
in the State, thanks to the inefficient bureaucracy by
which France was administered it was precisely this
craving for an unhazardous prosperity which had made
the middle classes the Revolutionaries of 1789.

It was natural that the class to which belonged country lawyers and doctors as well as bankers and merchants should long ago have grown restive under a régime thanks to which there was scarcely a respectability who might not become bankrupt merely because the government had not paid him what he was owed by it. Surely it was the first duty of the king to keep his contracts, to pay his debts, to administer methodically— in short, to be solvent, to *govern* ? And manifestly the king was not solvent, did not govern. Theoretically he was the central point of the elaborate centralisation which administered France. But in practice the bureaucratic machine functioned most irregularly, partly because its parts were out of order ; partly because its central spring had been failing ever since the reign of Louis XIV.

The king was not solvent and did not govern.[1] *The French Revolution was primarily a movement for order : a movement against chaos.* It was natural perhaps, since the 18th century worshipped reason, that its great Revolution should be a Revolution for rational administration. (And Poland, too, it should be noted, just as this time attempted its unhappy Revolution— for order too.) The intention was not to abolish centralisation—that came only with the Idealogues in 1790—still less to abolish the Crown—that came only after the king's treason in 1792. The intention was to create an efficient, instead of an inefficient, centralisation, to leave the Crown enough power to reform its own administration. The State must govern, said the physiocrat Mercier de la Rivière, " *suivant les règles de l'ordre essentiel* " ; scientifically, in fact ; that is all.

[1] For some account of the administrative system of the *ancien régime* v. infra, p. 65 foll.

But not only was the middle-class household invaded by all the discomforts that go with feeble government : it was increasingly distressed by its social inferiorities. As the Abbé Sieyès pointed out in his far-read pamphlet, the Third Estate provided church, law, army, government with nineteen-twentieths of the employed, and did all the onerous work ; only the lucrative and honourable places were reserved for the privileged. If the privileged orders were abolished, the nation, said Sieyès, would not be less than it is, but greater. Thus the army was commanded exclusively by men of noble birth : since 1781 even the promotion of non-commissioned officers (the Neys and Massénas of the future) had been forbidden. The diplomacy and the navy, too, were in the hands of the nobility. Whatever offices indeed took the eye or the imagination were reserved for the privileged. More than this : the enlightened middle classes felt themselves altogether unreasonably slighted. Barnave had seen his mother jostled at a theatre by a contemptuous noble. Such incidents have naturally not made their way into history in any number ; but they may have done far more towards opinion-making than the writings of Rousseau himself. *The Revolution was a movement for equality, against privilege.* Only indirectly was it aimed at the crown ; for just as the crown was intended to " reform despotism by the methods of despotism," so it was intended to retain power enough to destroy the privilege of the nobility. The middle classes had, as a matter of fact, no such urgent need as had the peasants to abolish that privilege. For, as we shall see, the feudal privilege of the noble (in relation to the peasant) was a thousand times more oppressive than his social privilege (in relation to the middle classes). But since the middle classes were politically conscious while the peasants suffered and were silent, it is the apparently insignificant grievance of the middle classes against privilege that is at the moment important for us.

The need for financial and administrative order, the passion for equality (we are still speaking only of the middle classes)—and yet are these by themselves enough to account for Revolution ? Consider : in the last decades of the old order not only had administration become more enterprising and more humane, but individual citizens had become enormously more prosperous. Why then did the Revolution come precisely when it did ? And why did it come more quickly and more directly (de Tocqueville asks this) precisely in those parts of France, the districts near Paris for example, where most progress had been made ? And why, conversely, did it take least hold precisely in those parts of France, in Poitou and Brittany for example, where the old order had least improved, where the *syndic* had remained most arbitrary and most violent ?

One answer, no doubt, is the answer we have given : that his increasing wealth itself had made the citizen increasingly dissatisfied with the insecurity of this new prosperity. But that answer by itself is not enough ; the need to stabilise and consolidate property did much ; but to answer our question, there are to be found formulas more illuminating and applicable universally ; not only, like this one, to the particular circumstances of France. The first, the brilliance of de Tocqueville has already made familiar. *The most dangerous moment for an oppressive government is the moment at which it begins to reform.* Why ? Because there are evils which are tolerable only so long as they appear inevitable. A man will suffer oppression uncomplaining, as he suffers the mountain which shuts the sun from his window—so long as he supposes that the oppression is as much part of an unalterable system as the mountain. Once let some trifling reform suggest to him that the whole system can be modified or destroyed, that mountains *can* be moved, and there is your revolutionary ready made.

And this was precisely what had happened in France. Louis XVI had been above all a reformer ; and that was his undoing. This was " the era of repentant monarchy," a brilliant phrase of Lord Acton's. And monarchy cannot afford to repent. Turgot, Malesherbes, Necker ; an apostle of progress, a benevolent intellectual, a genial, scientific banker ; there was a dangerous trio of ministers for a despot. Religious toleration, the abolition of torture, the emancipation of serfs on the crown estates, local self-government, Habeas Corpus, freedom of the press—all these, in greater or less degree, Louis XVI had accorded before the summons of the States-General, and the summons itself was to carry with it manhood suffrage, the right of initiating legislation and voting supplies, double representation of the Commons and the responsibility of ministers. Yes, Louis XVI was a reformer ; and the *ancien régime* in 1789 was at its most enlightened. Which was precisely why it fell. For the Revolution (it has been said) was not directed against Louis XVI at all : it was directed against Louis XIV, *le roi soleil*, and Louis XV of the *parc aux cerfs*.

But I must add here—in further answer to that question : Why did the Revolution come precisely when it did ?—a second answer, like this of de Tocqueville's of universal application, yet somewhat more precise in form. *In any society the revolutionaries will*

come from the class which is already acquiring power.
Power is poison in a sense other than Fénélon's. The
first taste of power infects always with a craving for
more. For of all drugs power is the most insidious.
Revolutions do not come from the down-trodden.
Revolutions come from those who have newly tasted
power and find that it is good. The Revolution of 1789,
like the war of 1914, came not because its authors were
oppressed, as at the time, like the German people, they
believed, but because, like the German people, they had
tasted, and desired, power.

The middle classes then were already acquiring power.
How ? And here for the first time we shall perhaps find
some evidence of the sort for which we said at the outset
we should be on the look out. " The middle classes "
(we said) " first neglecting and then using the miseries
of the politically unconscious masses for their own
deliberate assault upon power and privilege " : this was
the process of which in a less intense and rapid form we
hoped to find traces on the further side of 1789, as
evidence of the continuous existence of the Revolution
long before what we are accustomed to call its outbreak.
First then, the first stage of their encroachment upon
power, the neglect of the middle classes for the sufferings
of the peasant, their perpetual effort to dissociate
themselves from him is everywhere discernible.

In 1789 the middle classes were concentrated almost
exclusively in the towns. For a long while they had been
moving steadily from the countryside. And why ?
Because in the towns they could largely diminish or
evade altogether the burden of the *taille*, a direct tax
of rather more than fifty per cent. In the villages of
the countryside no one who was not of gentle birth
could escape it. And consequently so soon as the

villager, with the secular thriftiness of the French poor, had amassed his little competence, he removed to the shelter of the nearest town. And there he developed (as men will for the class from which they climb) the bitterest hostility and contempt for the peasant, whom he had left to bear unaided the monstrous burden of the *taille*. For three centuries the policy of the French crown had tended to deprive of their political rights *le menu peuple*, the poor : and the middle classes had only too frequently supported, had even sometimes suggested, this long encroachment. De Tocqueville illustrates from the answer of certain municipal officers to the inquiries of an *intendant* at the time of the municipal reform of 1764 this fatal instinct for concentrating in fewer and fewer hands what remained of such rights as that of electing magistrates.

And inevitably, once established in his country town, new interests and new ambitions claimed the refugee— it became his dearest desire to obtain a place under the government. Petty government appointments were continually being created to satisfy this appetite. (We have seen that this was but one of the ways in which the citizen was being brought into direct relation with the government, and given a direct personal interest in its solvency.) And these petty appointments carried with them immunities too, from one or other of the feudal burdens. The middle classes had established a privilege also in the sphere of Justice. The peasant could be arrested on the order of the *intendant*, and judged summarily and without appeal. For the middle classes on the other hand formal processes, lengthy and public trial.

And while they had thus been fastidious to disentangle themselves as best they could from the miseries of the

poor—one aspect of the twofold process which we are
tracing—the middle classes had been for a long while
encroaching upon *power*. That they were becoming
wealthy we have seen, and in all societies wealth is power.
They were becoming enlightened too. But, and this was
dangerous, they had administered. The *conseil du roi*,
in effect the ultimate authority of the kingdom, was a
body of indefinite, and therefore very formidable,
powers. Theoretically it had no jurisdiction ; for
theoretically it was the king, and the king alone, who
governed ; and the *conseil* did but advise. Actually,
and under Louis XVI, it was at once the Supreme Court
of Justice, the supreme administrative, legislative, and
fiscal tribunal. And its members came largely from the
middle classes. It worked, as became it, obscurely and
without recognition. Incredible that a system should
endure which gave to a yet powerful and unprivileged
class a taste so poignant of privilege and power !

The *intendant* was supreme agent of the government
in his own province. (" *Ce royaume de France est gouverné
par trente intendants* " said Law, the banker.) And the
intendant was usually of the middle classes, lately
ennobled. The *subdélégué*, his subordinate, was always
of unprivileged birth.

Lastly, the opposition of the middle class *Parlements*
to the crown in the last decades of the old order is at
once proof of the growing and restive sense of power
of the middle classes and a sort of rehearsal of the early
stages of the Revolution itself, evidence in fact that the
Revolution, as we have said, was in being before 1789.
Originally a supreme court of judicature but increasingly
political in character since the disuse of the States-
General, and now almost the only check on despotism,
the *Parlement* was at this time recruited principally from

the richer members of the middle classes. It had been re-established by Louis XVI, after its suspension by his predecessor, and had ever since been in opposition to the crown, or rather to the ministers of the crown. It had claimed to derive its powers from the people, not the king : already in 1759 the Parlement of Paris was talking of the " rights of the nation " in the true jargon of the States-General ; and though the real concern of the Parlement was its own privilege, it had been popular, and its protests and pamphlets had had a wide circulation. In the final quarrel of 1787 and 1788 it had had the temerity to declare null and illegal certain acts of royal authority, a temerity alarmingly supported by seditious outbreaks all over the country ; and its members even swore, when threatened with suppression, never to sit in any assembly other than the Parlement itself. The whole struggle closely examined is the most remarkable forecast of the sublime mulishness of the Third Estate in the States-General ; even the oath of the tennis court had there (in the oath to sit in no other assembly) its counterpart. It would be interesting to work out in detail an analogy between these pompous Parlements and the States-General : remembering always that by the side of the moribund institutions of a stricken society there will almost always be found growing the embryo of the institutions which are to take their place. *A movement for order and equality, brought to its crucial moment, partly because a despotic government had begun to reform, partly because a new class was tasting power.*

And before we leave the middle classes something must be said of the authors whom through these years they were reading and discussing. I want to speak of these writers very briefly and as apostles of that instinct

for order and equality which we have already traced.
Too much has been made of their influence ; for writers
always like to think that writers are important. But
in truth a writer is in the profoundest sense the product
of his age. A writer never gives to the world a *new* idea.
Either he has no audience or he is the creature of his
audience ; and the only thinker who ever contrived to
force a *new* idea upon the attention of his public was
crucified by it. Humanly speaking, ideas do not spring
ready armoured from their creator's brains. Writers,
and thinkers for that matter, are but the vulgarizers of
ideas ; they gather up and summarize and make hard
and luminous and concise the thoughts that are moving
dimly through the minds of many men. The writers of
the eighteenth century heralded the Revolution, but
they did not originate it. They were rather its effect
than its cause.

The *Economists* or *Physiocrats* of the middle of the
century are perhaps the most important of these
interpreters and heralds of the Revolution. Letronne,
Quesnay, Bodeau, de la Rivière (whose " *L'ordre naturel
et essentiel des sociétés politiques* " of 1767 conveniently
summarizes the Physiocrat views), Turgot, the elder
Mirabeau, these were men with tidy minds and a genius
for minding other people's business ; and they concerned
themselves not with abstract thinking but with matters
of financial administration. One may say that they
were the Fabians of their day. They wanted *scientific*
government, not liberty, for what could be more
haphazard and unscientific than liberty ? The un-
methodical—this was for them the mark of the beast :
" *tout semble y avoir été fait au hasard*," said Letronne,
wishing to damn irrevocably the past of France. It
was not a quickening of sympathy that moved them.

If they objected to the feudal system of taxation it was
because it was irrational that all the rich should be
exempt, or nearly exempt, from contributing to the
national income, not because they felt keenly the miseries
of the poor, which were inevitable if they were to fill the
royal exchequer all but alone. A scientific despotism
instead of an unscientific, this was their desire—a
business government, that perpetually recurrent and
disastrous ideal. They could admire even Frederic the
Great. And clearly the advent of order, of scientific
government, meant the advent of a scientific governing
class. And where was that new, scientific governing
class to be found ? Among the middle classes, said the
middle classes. And, further, method implied symmetry.
Above all, government must be rational. The diversity,
the irrational variety of privilege, incensed them
profoundly. Rather, far rather, uniform servitude than
heterogeneous liberty.

Order and equality then were the principal conclusions
of these Fabians of the eighteenth century. We need
say no more of them here. In the Idealogues and the
Declaration of Rights they live again.

Among the *philosophers* of the eighteenth century
(whose concern is rather with ideas than with administration) there are greater names, no doubt, than among the
physiocrats. But I doubt whether they are more
important to the understanding of the Revolution.
Their teaching at any rate does not so concisely forecast
the doctrines of the early Revolution. It is profounder
and of wider relevance of course and within it are to be
found almost all the ideas, and fragments of ideas,
which agitated the men of '89 and the men of '93. Some
of these philosophers we shall come upon later. There
is no need to consider at this stage even Rousseau, that

sublime sentimentalist, and his natural right. (And, after all, even Rousseau, like the rest, was a herald, not an author of the Revolution.)

Let us for the moment only notice the one obvious, most common characteristic of all the philosophers— rationalism. And in practice, observe, the rule of reason (which is fatal to so much that is precious) is fatal at any rate to disorder and to privilege.

Beyond this, it is worth while remembering first that without exception the philosophers (even Voltaire) were monarchists. They were not republican; they were for monarchy, but for a reformed and chastened monarchy; a democracy ruling through a king, rather than a king ruling over a democracy. And secondly, it is worth observing, for it is not always observed, and we shall see its importance soon, that in the writings of some of them—and notably of Turgot, who was a philosopher as well as a physiocrat—now first appeared the new creed of Optimism, the cult of Progress. Mankind, thought Turgot, marches ever forward, a theory which, combined with the pessimistic onslaught of Rousseau on Constitutions as such, became infinitely dangerous in the hands of Condorcet and the Idealogues of 1789. For man, they deduced, has but to cut himself loose from the fetters of established institutions and there is nothing he cannot achieve.

The diffusion of current ideas by physiocrat and philosopher affected of course every class in the community, save the peasant, who came under its influence only indirectly and when, at the very eve of Revolution, it was to the interest of the middle classes to instruct him how to draw up his *cahier* and to vote patriotically; that is to say, in the interest of the middle classes. I have spoken of these ideas here in relation primarily

to the middle classes, because since the middle classes,
we say, made the Revolution, we are principally concerned with the influences which assailed and moulded
them. It stands to reason that of these influences there
are some, perhaps not unimportant, which I have not
so much as mentioned—the American Revolution for
example. Now the example of the *fait accompli* in
America undoubtedly encouraged and inflamed France,
and the two Revolutions shared, it is true, very many
of their theories. But we are attempting an analysis
of the essential causes of the French Revolution, not an
exhaustive catalogue of its contributory influences.
And the French Revolution would have come as certainly
if the American colonists had never dreamed revolt.

I have spoken of the assault. Before we turn to that
vast section of the community which,though soon to be
of the assault, was, broadly speaking, for the moment
neutral, indifferent, content to suffer in silence, we will
consider briefly that part which, broadly speaking, was,
or should have been, upon the defensive. I say *should
have been,* for although, as we have seen, the privilege
of the noble was to be one of the principal objects of
assault, it is remarkable that no one welcomed the
summons of the States-General more joyfully than the
nobility. For the nobles too believed themselves to have
a grievance against despotism. Order they also desired ;
and as for equality they had not clearly thought out
what that would mean.

The nobility of France was in 1789 in the most
dangerous situation conceivable : for it had lost power
but retained privilege. Ever since the close of the Fronde
in 1653 the policy of the French crown had been to
undermine the power of the feudal lords. The feudal
owner no longer governed. In the old days the feudal

burdens had been grievous, it is true, but in return
for them it had been the noble who had guaranteed
society. All that remained of his power, his *service* to
society, in the eighteenth century was the limited
dispensation of justice and control of police within his
own *seigneurie*—both considered by this time as a source
of revenue rather than a public duty. In fact he no
longer rendered any service in return for his privilege.
And the privilege remained ; crushing the peasant
(feudal dues) ; exasperating the middle classes (social
monopoly) ; ruining the nation (exemption from taxation). The power of the noble had declined with his
withdrawal from the countryside, and it had been the
almost continuous policy of the crown to withdraw
him from his estates to some office about the court.
The tradition grew that honour demanded that the
noble's place should be near the fountain of honour,
the king. And so the feudal landlord became an
absentee. When indeed in the eighteenth century the
danger of this process was suspected the government
was unable to arrest it. For, shorn of power, life in the
country was not attractive enough to keep the noble
from Versailles. And so he was slowly divorced from the
people he had once led and judged and protected.

But the feudal privileges remained. Monopolies, tolls
and dues of astonishing extent and variety, and the
exemptions from taxation—the nobles paid now (when
they did not avoid them) poll tax and *vingtième*, but not
the most crushing of the taxes, not the *taille*—all these
he might once have claimed at any rate to earn ; but
they remained to him now that he could not conceivably
claim to be earning them any longer. And though, we
have said, what initiated the movement for equality was
the merely social privilege of the noble, in relation to the

middle classes, yet, we shall see, what gave the Revolution impetus, and, afterwards, direction, was just this oppressive feudal privilege in relation to the peasant. The nobles, as a class, the hundred thousand of them, were neither unintelligent nor (grossly) immoral ; but *they retained privilege without power* ; that was their principal folly and their principal crime, and that is the essential truth about them. But it will be observed also that mere separation, the transplanting of the noble to Versailles, not only his oppressive privilege, had estranged him from the peasant. It was in la Vendée and Brittany that more than elsewhere lords lived upon their estates and it was in la Vendée and Brittany that the old order died hardest. For familiarity is sometimes as efficient a preservative as affection.

The clergy of France were partly, like the nobles, of the privileged; partly, like the middle classes and the peasant, of the unprivileged ; and among the unprivileged many, with the middle classes, were of the assault.

As an order the clergy owned perhaps a fifth of the soil of France, and a yearly income from land, invested property, tithes and various fees of more than two hundred and fifty million livres. Naturally this wealth was most unequally distributed. The archbishoprics and bishoprics, of which there were a hundred and fifty, were almost wholly reserved for men of noble birth, very often pluralists, whose income might reach two hundred thousand, or in one case, four hundred thousand livres a year. These with the powerful courtier-rulers of the various religious orders were the privileged. The *curé* (or vicar), on the other hand, received not less than seven hundred livres in 1789, and the *vicaire* (or curate) half that amount.

Moreover, while the prelate was often an absentee and a courtier, the parish priest was of, and among, the

people, seeing, and sharing sometimes, their distress.
The parish priests, unprivileged like the middle classes,
shared often the enlightenment of the middle classes
without their divorce from the humble. (Twenty-four
of forty names on two lists of subscribers to the Encyclopædia discovered in Périgord are those of parish priests).
And accordingly, until many of them had been made
enemies by its assault upon the faith, among the parish
priests were to be found some of the sturdiest champions
of the Revolution. And in 1789 the *cahiers* of the clergy
were as radical in their demands as those of the *tiers
état* : they were as whole-hearted for the supremacy of
the States-General : they were as loud for liberty and
equality. It was not long before they came to regret
these enthusiasms.

And those who suffered in silence ? In many ways,
it is true, the lot of the French peasant in the eighteenth
century was less intolerable than ever before. The decree
of 1774 had abolished serfdom upon the royal estates,
and had encouraged other feudal owners to abolish it
too. The fall in the value of money had lightened the
burden of the money dues, which remained unaltered
in amount. More than this, *the peasant was getting
possession of the land.* He owned already perhaps a
third of the soil of France (to the astonishment of Arthur
Young). Indeed M. Loutchisky has lately shown by an
analysis of 128 parishes in Limousin that on the eve of
the Revolution more than half of their soil was owned
by small peasant proprietors, and that in the districts
he studied not more than seventeen per cent. of the
peasants were landless. But, like the middle classes'
taste of power, all this did but whet his appetite for
what might be if he were once freed from his crushing
burdens. And with how terrible a patience he acquired

his land ! He ate miserably, clothed himself in harsh, coarse stuffs, knew not the smallest luxuries, tolerated all things, until at last the tiny nook of soil is his, and each year his heart is buried in it again with the seed. But to own the soil instead of tilling it merely meant that he felt all the more crushingly the feudal dues. Now all their weight, not part only, rests upon his patient shoulders. The *corvée* (forced labour) takes him from the well-loved plot (which for all his labour will scarcely keep his family alive) to work elsewhere unpaid. The noble's game must spoil, unmolested, the crops he has so hardly grown. He cannot sell his produce in the market without further dues to the noble, nor grind nor cook his grain save in the noble's mill and the noble's oven. The feudal rights squeezed the peasant in the interests of an absentee landlord who spent his unearned profits on fine clothes at Versailles : the exemptions of the privileged in taxation fleeced him in the interest of the privileged and of high policies of state which he had no voice in framing and which did him no good and often harm.

The monarchy of Louis XVI was a repentant monarchy, but the burden had not yet lightened sufficiently, the timidly civilizing government of Louis XVI had not yet civilized far enough, to make the peasant vocal or self-assertive. The peasant was terribly oppressed, and it is not, as I said, the oppressed who revolt. And the *corvée*, the *taille* (which had perhaps decupled in two hundred years), and conscription were still enough to freeze the miserable into the most satisfactory docility, and but for the middle classes each of the millions of peasants would have continued, for yet many decades, to contribute, in Anatole France's phrase, by his private misery to the general welfare of all.

Did the miserable then contribute nothing to up-heaval? No, it is true, they played some small part even in the preparation of the outbreak. For the middle classes (for their own purposes) had begun to educate them. The catchwords of the eighteenth century—natural rights, contracts and the rest of them—must for some decades have hovered vague, bewildering, sug-gestive though, across the mental horizons of many peasants. But that was of little moment. It was only when it was a question of compiling the *cahiers*—that there began something like an active propaganda among the peasants. These *cahiers* were the petitions and remonstrances drawn up by the electors of France as instructions to their deputies at the coming States-General. And the villagers despatched their *cahiers*, for the villagers had their vote. Why? This is extremely important. Why did the Notables desire, and the Court approve, a suffrage to include every Frenchman twenty-five years old and entered on the tax rolls? For, observe, this was a more democratic suffrage than France was, save once, ever to have courage for during the first Revolution again. Why then did notable persons encourage so hazardous a gift to France of the *ancien régime*? *Because the threat came, and was seen to come, from the middle classes, the well-to-do.* Would not notable persons then be prudent to dilute the influence of the restive, unprivileged, well-to-do with the indifference of the patient, unnumbered miserable? Would not, incidentally, the feudal influence of the noble still pater-nally direct the activities of his own peasants? It was a stratagem which we shall see repeated when the *ancien régime*, once conquered, was fighting desperately under Louis XVIII for its restoration. Still, the miserable has his vote. Then must we not educate the miserable, reflect the restive well-to-do ? Certainly we must educate them. And the process of education is embalmed in the *cahiers*. The *cahiers* of the Third Estate, even the primary *cahiers* of the villages, before they had been consolidated for the intermediate assemblies or electoral districts, clearly came often from a middle-class pen. Many of them are the same : the Abbé Sieyès, for one, distributed a celebrated model, which was widely adopted, often with addition to its sonorous political speculation of some more homely and individual distress ; as when the peasants of Champagne suggest mildly that their dogs might be graciously released from the logs fastened to their collars to prevent them from running after the lord's game.

In their own interests the middle classes were educating the miserable. And educators teach always more than they suspect. July the fourteenth first suggested that this education might one day prove to have had dangerous pupils. The fourteenth of July has been persistently misunderstood. It has been taken for much the greatest and the best event in history ; and it has been taken for a mere cruel and accidental riot. But it was neither ; or both. The taking of the Bastille was not the work of the revolutionaries—that is clear. The revolutionaries were at Versailles, talking. And the *tocsin* which rang out that fourteenth of July was not rung as it rang on later and organised days of riot—to call the insurgents to arms ; it was the wild cry of alarm of the well-to-do of Paris sent out because the robbers were coming to town. And the victors of the Bastille *were* robbers ; and at the first news of its fall the Revolution-making respectabilities of the States-General at Versailles were as confounded as the Court itself. But not for long. Within a few hours they had

accepted, and, more, adopted, the deed accomplished,
and the legend of the Bastille had taken already the
niche it has filled ever since, highest in the temple of
Revolution. Very soon the respectabilities were convinced that they had captured the Bastille themselves.
For the fall of the Bastille meant the surrender of the
Court, which up to that moment had had good hope of
overwhelming the Revolution of words at Versailles.
October 6th, the transference of the Royal family (and
therefore of the Assembly) to Paris was the inevitable
sequel of July 14th. And of how much more than this
was July 14th not the initiation! The hegemony
of Paris over the Revolution ; direct government by
the Commune of Paris (one day to be democratic as
well as direct) instead of indirect government by the
deputies of the assembly : the power of the National
Guard. Of all these things July 14th was the cause
direct. But indirectly its significance was greater far.
For it was the herald of the second Revolution. For the
moment this illegitimate offspring, adopted by the
middle classes and the first Revolution, merely helped
to establish their new oligarchy. But for all that it was
a portent of what was three years later, for once and
for a little while, to overthrow that oligarchy—the
miserable.

And meanwhile the miserable were being educated.
For the moment they had not profited fully by their
lesson—July fourteenth showed merely, had there been
eyes to see, that they might one day be dangerous
students. And it was not till 1792 that the lesson showed
itself fully and terribly learned, and that the educators
suffered the common fortune of their kind and found
that they had taught their pupils what they did not
believe themselves.

CHAPTER II

MIRABEAU AND THE IDEALOGUES

So much for the outbreak, which was not an outbreak but a continued process. So much for the teachers, teaching what they did not suspect. Let us now regard the Revolution, arrested, as it were, at its next most critical moment.

And to that moment a personality has some importance. One must beware of personalities. Even now something lingers of the Carlyle tradition that the history of this Revolution is a gallery of personalities : that the Revolution was the work of great men. Great men are a myth : there are none. Most of what has been deduced from the orthodox theory of Evolution is, no doubt, false : but it is at least clear that humanity does not progress, if it progresses, in a rise and fall from isolated pinnacle to pinnacle of individual greatness, but in a steady ascent. Our war, for example, produced no great men : only great peoples. Men we have called great in history are men who summed, or stood for, the soul of a people or an age. Cromwell was great in so far as he stood for the Puritan idea, the younger Pitt for England unconquerable. And in the ten years after 1789 France had no single soul. She was torn by too many conflicting creeds and passions : it was not till after 1799 that her inveterate passion for glory united her, and becoming incarnate in Napoleon made him for a little while into what we call a great man.

The elements of the arrested moment I want to consider now are two : Mirabeau and the Idealogues. Or, to put it more elaborately, I want to show shortly how the oligarchic and artificial settlement imposed in their own interest by the middle classes, after the triumph prepared by themselves but made possible by the nameless on July fourteenth and October sixth, was seen to be impermanent (because artificial) as well as unjust (because oligarchic) by one man, who could not bear to think that he should have contributed merely to a great destruction ; how for eighteen months he offered a solution which, by abolishing the new oligarchy of privilege, would consolidate and make lasting what was just and *real* in the achievement hitherto of the Revolution (which had just destroyed the old oligarchy of privilege) ; and so forestall the Terror and Napoleon himself ; how, and more particularly why, his solution failed ; and how its failure was at once the tragedy and the explanation of the first Revolution.

Now it is just possible that this solution failed not because the solution was inadequate, but because its author was Mirabeau, and his past Mirabeau's past. And this is why personality becomes transiently our concern.

Not that we need trouble ourselves here with the not unhumorous tangle of intrigue and debt in which Mirabeau was pleased to involve himself until the year 1789. Enough that he did emerge upon the stage of the Revolution with an altogether unsavoury record, a record to be legitimately sniffed at by orthodoxy. To nine out of ten of the respectabilities of the States-General here was a man who overdid things (La Marck has recorded his first meeting with Mirabeau, his extravagant dress, low bows, and egregious compliments) ; no gentleman this, blatant, *a man not to be trusted*. So much the Mouniers and the Lafayettes could see ; so much the Mouniers and the Lafayettes of this world always do see. But they saw no more than this. Yet beneath his blatancy Mirabeau was possessed of that rarest of all gifts, insight into the nature of things, where the Mouniers and the Lafayettes saw only their appearances. There are few enough who can thus detect *reality* even in the old past : far fewer are those who can see it in the event as it unfolds.

Mirabeau emerges then upon the stage of 1789 with the reputation of a rogue and a flair for reality. And what was the world in which he found himself ? A world of Idealogues.

A world of Idealogues ! Now so much in the next three years is inexplicable but for the Idealogues that it is important to suggest some conception of their mental disposition.

Two elements go to the mental composition of an Idealogue : an intellectual temper common among his countrymen then and now, and a philosophic prejudice peculiar to his own time. Temperamentally an Idealogue is a man who arrives at, or accepts, generalisations without a study of particulars, builds his pyramid, as it were, from the apex downward and so applies *a priori* principles to politics. This is a student's, an academic blindness : metaphysicians Bonaparte slightingly called the Idealogues, but they have always been common in his France. There is a blindness too of the practical man (the blindness perhaps of our country) who is industrious among his particulars without suspicion that general truths can come of them. Whether the academic or the

practical blindness is more dangerous to politics I will
not try to say. But the academic blindness *is* dangerous,
and when, as in 1789, it afflicts a whole people, profoundly dangerous. The Idealogues accepted their
general principles ready-made from Rousseau and the
rest; and if they appeared to conflict with experience
the Idealogues concluded that it was experience which
was at fault. And thus these happy world-regenerators
were untroubled by doubt, and all their contradictory
decrees were equally infallible. It is so easy to pronounce
(for example) that France, freed of the old order, will
renounce the idea of conquest; that villages, left to
themselves ungoverned, will order themselves for the best.
(And so incredible that any man who knew anything
of the history of France could believe such things.)

Now this excessive confidence in abstract principles
the Idealogues shared with Frenchmen of other times
and other kinds, but for all that Ideology was a distinctive and transient phase of thought. For upon the
inexhaustible fertility of this national disposition to
apriorism, untempered by the mingling with affairs
which local self-government would have brought a
happier country, was sown the dragon seed of the
eighteenth century philosophers. Man progresses, proclaimed Turgot: the new gains always on the old,
we do not recede continually (as so many centuries had
believed) from the golden age: the golden age lies
ahead of us, nearer every year. Natural man is corrupted by customs and laws, thought Rousseau.

One theory persuaded the Idealogues of the infinite
perfectibility of man; the other suggested that the
destruction of institutions was the high road towards
that perfectibility, for to destroy institutions was to
strike off the artificial fetters from the limbs of the

natural man. All then we have to do, concluded the
Idealogues, is to break irretrievably with our past.
Man shall be born again : he need but renounce the
heresies of the old time and the great age begins
anew.

Very much of the course the Revolution took is due
to the Idealogues. For confident in their regeneration
of man they did contrive, notably in diplomacy and
local government, artificially to stifle instinct, to effect
for a little while a cleavage with the age-long tradition
of France. So that, as we shall see, more than has been
suspected of the agony of the Revolution was spent in
the unconscious return to the traditional, instinctive
methods ; to the tradition of glory instead of peace,
the tradition of strong centralised government instead of
liberty.

Such were the Idealogues ; untrained in affairs ;
believers in general principles not based upon examined
facts. And such, naturally, was the Idealogue National
Assembly : where the speeches were long-winded essays
read inexorably through even when the argument
they proffered had been answered long ago ; with endless
logomachy over trifles, yielding now and again to hours
of headlong, tear-mingled enthusiasms such as that of
August fourth, which would profess to sweep away
unconsidered in twenty-four hours the achievement of
centuries.

And from the Idealogue assembly what was emerging ?
Not only unreality (the artificial rupture with tradition)
but privilege. A constitution of 1791, which, after the
Declaration of Rights had trumpeted equality and
universal suffrage, reserved the election of deputies for
the prosperous who paid in direct taxes the equivalent
of ten days' work, and even the illusory suffrage in the

first degree for those who paid the equivalent of three
days' work, while membership of the Assembly itself
was confined to those who paid the *marc d'argent* (fifty
livres) in direct taxes and owned some landed property—
so that, as Camille Desmoulins observed bitterly in the
Révolutions de France, neither Corneille, Mably, nor
Rousseau himself would have been eligible as deputies.
These were the " active citizens." The poor were
" passive citizens "—citizens, that is, without the rights
of citizenship. The suspensive veto, too, ensured that
the king (who might perhaps ally himself with the poor)
could check the legislation of the Assembly for no more
than one session. A Civil Constitution of the clergy, too,
was emerging which, leaving only spiritual supremacy
to the Pope, created an independent Gallican church,
with equalised dioceses and bishops and vicars chosen
by the " active citizens."

It should be noticed that this creation of privilege
was a betrayal of the excluded in a twofold sense. It
was a betrayal because the Declaration of Rights had
promised Equality : and it was a betrayal because, as
we have seen, but for the excluded, and what the excluded had done on July 14th and October 6th, there
would by this time have been no Revolution in being.
Not only, that is, had the middle classes promised
equality to the excluded, but they owed them equality
even if the promise had never been made. Loustallot
meant something of this sort when he observed that in
truth the Revolution had been made possible by a few
patriots who had not the honour of sitting in the
National Assembly. Nor was the Constitution of '91
their only deception of the poor ; for though they proclaimed the abolition of feudalism so loud on August
fourth that they hoodwinked historians for generations,

they did in fact (M. Aulard has lately made this clear[1])
destroy only about one-third of the feudal burdens ; of
which the peasant (as we shall see later) was not finally
quit till 1793. The first Revolution then was ending
not in equality but in the substitution of the new
politically privileged, the middle classes, for the old
socially privileged, the nobles. And *order* (we shall see),
which the Idealogues hoped to establish by the indis-
criminate liberty granted to forty thousand communes,
was further off than under the *ancien régime*.

Mirabeau alone saw clearly that all this meant a
second Revolution, in which might be overwhelmed
the solid achievement of the first. Mirabeau alone saw
that at any cost the Revolution must be *determined*,
consolidated. " *J'ai voulu*," he said, " *préparer, accelerer,
déterminer peut-être une grande révolution dans les choses
humaines* "—to prepare, to accelerate, if it might be to
determine ! In the first two of his aims he succeeded :
his failure in the last and greatest is (we said) at once
the tragedy and the explanation of the first Revolution.

Mirabeau's formula, his scheme for the " determination " of the Revolution, never altered in essentials;
although the means by which he sought to achieve it
varied with circumstance. The formula is clear. *Le roi
se déclarerait populaire*—the king must ally himself with
the people against the new privileged, the middle classes,
as at the time of the Fronde he had allied with the people
against the once privileged, the nobles. For in the orgy
of rupture with tradition which came with the first years
of the Revolution the king too had his part. He was
disposed to ally himself " unhistorically " with the lost
cause of the nobles. This unhistoric alliance was to be
repeated by his brother, Charles the tenth : it cost

[1] Aulard : *La Révolution Française et la régime féodal.* 1919. v. infra p. 77 f.

both of them a throne, and the elder his life. And once
" historically " allied with the people the king must
announce that he accepted the Revolution as far as it
had gone—abolition (as it was thought) of feudalism,
destruction of privilege, limited monarchy. He must
break with the middle class assembly. (Later, when
many chances had gone by, this would mean leaving
Paris and appealing to the provinces against the capital
—presage of the quarrel of Jacobin and Gironde.) In
place of the all-powerful legislature, with a weak,
mistrusted ministry, there must go with the popular
monarchy a powerful executive responsible to, and
members of, a popular assembly. For Mirabeau censured
continually the paralysing lack of confidence between
the assembly and the ministers : without it, he said,
there could never be strong government.

Now the Declaration of Rights had declared (Article
Sixteen) that a state in which the legislature and the
executive were not separate possessed no Constitution.
The ministers must not, that is, sit in the assembly.
This strange but classic dogma of the " Separation of
Powers " was due partly to Rousseau,[1] partly to the
evil old traditions of the past—Were not these after all
the king's ministers, racy of the *ancien régime*? Mirabeau,
with his eyes on the English Constitution, had realised
that if there was ever to be strong government (and this
after all was the prime need of France), the executive
and the legislature must become one. The *Courrier de
Provence*, his organ, declared expressly (Sept. 11-14,
1789) : " Until our Constitution has undergone the test
of time, wise men will continue to admire in this England
practical results which are far superior to the sublime
theories of our Utopians. They will not cease to believe

[1] See, *e.g.*, *Du Contrat Social*, Book II, chap. 2.

that direct daily intercourse between the ministers and
the legislative body, such as takes place in the British
Parliament, is not only just and profitable, but necessary
and open to no objection whatever." Instructive,
unheeded protest of the realist among Idealogues !

Such, baldly, was the scheme. And there was support
for it too among those outside the assembly—they were
not many—who saw what the assembly had done.
Thus Loustallot in the *Révolutions de Paris*, November,
1789, appeals to the king against the *marc d'argent* and
the bourgeois oligarchy. Let the king say to the assembly
" The nation is sovereign, and I am its chief : you are
but its agents, and neither its masters nor mine."
(*Vous n'êtes que ses commissaires, et vous n'êtes ni ses
maîtres, ni les miens*). A *district* even, that of Henry fourth,
in December, 1789, desired to appeal to the king against
the *marc d'argent* (which foreshadowed Mirabeau's
scheme, the royal veto in the interest of the people).
Such was the plan. And the attempt to apply it,
Mirabeau's revolutionary career in fact, falls naturally
into two phases.

In the first, Mirabeau's instrument was the assembly.
He tried, tortuously of necessity, to establish there an
ascendancy, and with it his solution of the problem he
saw so plainly to need solving. The assembly would not
trust him. Here is an adventurer who would be vizier
and perhaps even dictator—so argued the assembly, not
without some justification, for now Mirabeau's past was
entering history. The end came on November 7th, when
Lanjuinais moved (*motion Lanjuinais*) that no member
of the assembly might receive place or pension from the
executive authority. It was the old dread of the
executive bred under the *ancien régime*, but, as Mirabeau
bitterly observed, the assembly might as well have

decreed that the disability should apply to Monsieur de
Mirabeau and to him alone. The resolution was in effect
a vote of no confidence in Mirabeau and his political
theories. If any one day made certain the fall of the
monarchy it was this. The first phase of Mirabeau's
effort had failed.

The assembly was the instrument of that first phase,
to which this motion of Lanjuinais put an end. The
instrument of the second was the court, approached
not by oratory but by the series of papers for which
the Comte de la Marck was intermediary and which
begin in May of 1790 (the interval between this and the
fiasco of November 7th being occupied by an unsuccessful
attempt to use the Comte de Provence, the king's
brother). These are the papers published, with Mirabeau's letters to La Marck and Lafayette, in 1851, and
for those who want one Mirabeau's Letters are the best
book on Mirabeau's political career that can be read.

In return for his support and advice Mirabeau's debts
were to be paid and he was to receive monthly 6,000
livres, besides bills to the amount of a million livres
if he was thought to have earned them at the session's
end. Too much has been said of Mirabeau's hire. His
own comment will suffice : " I was paid to be of my own
opinion." The essential opinion never altered : the
remedy for the sickness of the time remained the same :
only, the end, urged now upon the court in place of the
assembly, and with the urgence of a desperate situation
growing daily, necessarily needed somewhat other
means. It is true that for a while even in this second
phase of his attempt Mirabeau dallied with the methods
of his first, parliamentary government through a
constitutional majority in an assembly which, repealing
the *motion Lanjuinais*, should allow the king to place

in power some of the leaders of the left. ("A Jacobin
as minister is not a Jacobin minister.") But Lafayette,
the too respectable, was necessary for that plan, as well
as the recalcitrant, suspicious assembly, and the lingering
hopes of it faded. The new devices move less directly,
but to the same end. Sooner or later the assembly must
succumb to the discredit of its own vices and misjudg-
ments. Let us meanwhile multiply its occasions of
offence. And then, as time passes and still nothing done,
Mirabeau writes with more urgency, let the king leave
Paris and summon the assembly to his side in some
provincial town where the organised mob will no longer
overawe it. And if the assembly cannot or will not come
and civil war results—well, there are times when civil
war may be a blessing in disguise. Only at all costs
there must be no reaction ; the king must place himself
in the power of the provinces, not the provinces in the
power of the king. Even if a whole generation and the
memory of it could be obliterated, France could not
return to the *ancien régime*.

Such was the plan. We know that it failed. For one
thing, as Mirabeau remarked, there was only one man
at court and she was the queen. And the queen still
mistook the Revolution for a rebellion. Also here, too,
Mirabeau was not trusted.

*The king to accept the Revolution as far as it had gone,
and to ally himself with the people against the new oligarchy.
A strong executive responsible to and part of a popular
assembly.* Why was that scheme not accepted by France
of 1790 ? Did it fail for a mere accident, the accident of
Mirabeau's past, because its author was suspect ; or
was there in it some deeper inadequacy to the obscure
needs and stresses of that time ? That is the problem.

Perhaps the simplest, if not the most logical, method

of suggesting an answer to it will be to look ahead ten
years to what proved to be at last the permanent
achievements of the Revolution and then to consider
whether those achievements could have been guaranteed
by the state which Mirabeau imagined in 1790. Those
few but great achievements which endured, with which
France on the whole rested content, we will assume to
represent the essential needs of the country, so that,
if they had been satisfied in 1790, there need perhaps
have been no second Revolution in 1792. (And that
second phase of the Revolution, remember, was due to
the unconscious, more perhaps than to the explicit,
discomforts in the France of the first phase.)

Briefly, then, without more argument here, let us say
that, within France, the permanent achievement of the
Revolution, enduring under the first Empire, was twofold : Equality and Order. Other conquests the
Revolution proclaimed, these it achieved ; political
equality (with the transference of the land to the peasant)
and a strong centralised administration.

Could Mirabeau's solution have ensured these in 1790
or 1791 ? For if it could we are to conclude, we said,
that, probably at least, a mere chance, the suspect
personality of its author, not its own intrinsic weakness,
was the cause of its failure.

This is a matter for debate which cannot be debated
here. Let me only say that at least there is strong *prima
facie* argument for believing that Mirabeau's scheme,
thoroughly attempted, might have given France in 1790
or 1791 what she at last achieved ; without regicide,
without the Terror, without (perhaps) the war against
the world, without Napoleon. For Mirabeau's scheme,
we have seen, was expressly designed to strengthen the
administration and to abolish privilege. (And to

strengthen administration and abolish privilege were
with the panic of win-the-war and hunt-the-spy the
prime motives of the Terror.)

Logically then, according to our premise, it was
Mirabeau's personality that made the failure of Mirabeau's scheme. And this should be our conclusion.
But it is not. For there was a factor we did not consider
in the premise, and that was the Idealogue temperament.
No scheme, I think, could have *determined* the Revolution in 1790 or 1791, because France then was in the
hands of the Idealogues, and the Idealogues believed
with passion that France was upon the eve of a sublime
Monday morning, a new age. The mere suggestion that
the Revolution was a thing to be arrested, that so soon
it could have done all it would ever do for France, for
Man—this was in Idealogue eyes folly and heresy and
treachery to the state. France was to renounce the idea
of conquest, substitute liberty for government, and set
to all mankind the example of the brotherhood of man.
Inconceivable that she should pause here and now.
The Revolution in the hand of the Idealogues was bound
to go on. And it went on accordingly—over the bodies
of the Idealogues.

CHAPTER III

JACOBINISM

In spite of Mirabeau, the middle class oligarchy did not yield to the two principal forces which opposed it, the king and the dispossessed. And consequently in 1792 the middle class oligarchy came to a violent end. On April 20th, 1792, war had been declared on Austria. On August 10th the Tuileries were stormed and the king's functions suspended—by inviting Austrian assistance he had added to the folly of the " unhistoric alliance " the crime of treachery. The Legislative Assembly established manhood suffrage in place of the limited suffrage of 1791, and summoned a national convention to revise the Constitution. Thus ended the middle class oligarchy which had controlled the Revolution thus far. On Sept. 21st, 1792, royalty was abolished, and on January 21st, 1793, Louis XVI was executed. Through the next two years the Revolution becomes steadily more democratic. But as to this progress towards political equality there was no conflict : and the next two years are filled, not with any conflict as to the coming of democracy, but first with the struggle of the Jacobins of the so-called " Mountain " with the Gironde, then with a strange new phase of the Revolutionary idea—Jacobinism.

All history is universal ; but here more clearly than before we touch universal history. We deal, I mean,

with the sort of conflict, and the sort of tragedy, which
must come with revolutions of any time or place.

First, the struggle of the Gironde with the Mountain,
which extended, roughly, from the opening of the
National Convention in September, 1792, to the proscription of the Girondins on June 2nd of 1793. What
precisely was that issue ? Not merely, that is, the particular tactical decision reached, but the far-reaching
political principles at stake, an issue fundamental to
our own time too.

What were these *Girondins* ? First (what is always
easier to see in men), the things they were not.

M. Aulard reckons them roughly at 165. They did
not all come from the south. The Gironde itself returned,
besides eight Girondins, two deputies of the Mountain
and two of the Centre. Indeed, the label " Girondins "
would have meant very little to the Paris of 1792. It
owes its wide acceptance to Lamartine and his *Histoire
des Girondins* of 1847. " Brissotins " they would rather
have been called by the men of their own time, or
" Rolandistes." Lamartine, too, created the legend and
glamour of these Girondins.

They were not a political party. They shared no
agreed programme. The mere idea of a political programme revolted them, admitted Meillan : *la seule
pensée d'une démarche combinée nous révoltait.* A number
of them met fairly regularly at 5 Place Vendôme, that
is all.

They were not a political party. What held them
together then ? Primarily, I think, a spiritual affinity,
and, founded upon this, a political creed which never
amounted to a political programme. If one word is to
define the spiritual quality which was shared by the
Girondins we can only say that they were " remote."

They were remote, firstly, in the sense that they were fastidious—superior persons. *Les Girondins furent perdus par leur aristocratie d'attitude, de gouts, presque d'épiderme. Presque d'épiderme*, that is the truth about them (the brilliant and, I think, untranslatable phrase is M. Aulard's). Not that they were undemocratic. In theory they were more democratic than the Mountain ; Condorcet's project for the Constitution of 1793 was more, not less, democratic than that, which was adopted, of Herault de Séchelles. The people as a phrase in Rousseau, as a sentimental glow, a peroration, the Girondins understood and loved ; but the people swarming into the Salle du Manège, odorous, irrational, perilous to the sacrosanctity of its representatives—this they could not tolerate. And the people was invading the assembly more and more. John Moore, an Englishman in Paris in the summer of 1792, records how in early August he watched the crowd in the galleries of the Manège insulting and threatening and shouting down the members of the assembly. " I expected, of course," he observes, " that the galleries would be cleared," but he was soon convinced " that it was more likely that the people in the galleries should thrust out the members, than that the members would expel them."[1] Even in his *Mémoires* it is with a visible shudder that Buzot recalls " their hideous, muddy faces, black or copper-coloured, and deep-sunken eyes . . . their stinking breath " (" *leurs vilaines figures boueuses, noires ou couleur de cuivre . . . avec des yeux enfoncés à mi-tête . . . leurs huleines nauseabondes.*")[2] The theorist of popular government inadvertently encountering the

[1] *Journal during a residence in France* by John Moore, M.D. (pub. 1793). Vol. I, p. 26.
[2] Buzot : *Mémoires*, p. 57 (edn. 1866).

people is a tragi-comedy which belongs to all ages. This sentimental fastidiousness was to some extent recognised by contemporaries. And no doubt the deliberate filthiness of Marat's personal appearance was intended to be to some extent symbolical.

And the Girondins were remote, secondly, in the academic way ; they were remote from reality, the survival of the Idealogue temperament when the hour of the Idealogue temperament had passed. The war was at its outset a Girondin war, and though it is true it was, as Brissot avowed, an intrigue against the monarchy, there is no doubt that the Girondin enthusiasm for it was very largely what may be called Idealogue enthusiasm for a war which was to introduce the golden age, and after which, in Isnard's phrase, would dawn on Europe, *le jour de la philosophie.* The Girondins understood ideas, not men, or even things. They were phrase-makers. Levasseur de la Sarthe speaks scornfully of their " empty phrases." " When they wanted anything practical organised," he remarks of the Marsh or Centre of the Convention, " they came to us " (the Mountain). " They realised that organisation was impossible with men like Louvet, Isnard or even Vergniaud."[1] Of the Gironde, too, might have been made Catherine's observation to Diderot : *Vous ne travaillez que sur le papier, qui souffre tout.*

From these moral and intellectual predispositions, which held the Gironde loosely together, pretty obviously resulted the political creed which they shared. And this is the normal sequence. The opinion, the act even, comes first, determined by unconscious motives. It is followed by the explicit creed, which justifies it. All their prejudices bade them mistrust and fear the people in the

[1] Levasseur de la Sarthe : *Mémoires,* I, p. 25, 1829.

flesh, and the people in the flesh, the Revolutionary
Commune of Paris, had begun, before the meeting
of the Convention, to threaten dictatorship over the
National Assembly. The Revolutionary Commune
formed itself, thanks to Danton, on the evening of
August 9th, 1792 ; and after the insurrection of August
10th it was the Revolutionary Commune which transformed the suspension of the king and his lodgment in
private quarters in the Luxembourg (which was what the
Assembly had intended) into strict imprisonment and
the end of the monarchy. *" When the people puts itself
into a state of insurrection it revokes all powers and takes
them to itself"* was the reply of the Revolutionary
Commune on August 9th to the protest of the Council
General of the Commune which it was violently super-
seding. In this new principle lay unimagined possibilities.
But indeed that the people of Paris were determined to
over-ride and browbeat their deputies there had been
plenty of evidence before the self-creation of the
Revolutionary Commune had provided the instinct
with the rudiments of a more definite mechanism.
Since 1790 the Jacobin club, we shall see, had been a
forcing house for public opinion and the deputies in the
Assembly had learned to listen deferentially to its
instructions. " How can men be brought to deliberate
or vote with freedom," demands the worthy Moore, "
who are pursued, insulted and menaced by a mob for
the opinions and votes they give ? "

In September, 1792, the Girondins could not guess
all that was to grow from that new principle, but already
they suspected and feared it. Was a ridiculously small
minority to browbeat the representatives of the people ?
The political creed of the Girondins was in essence a
theory of representation. Theirs was the classical theory

of representation, Burke's theory; that, once chosen, the elected person must be left free to exercise uncontrolled his own discretion. Until his constituents are next invited to an election his powers are in fact irrevocable and the majesty of the people becomes in practice the majesty of the representatives of the people.

And so, standing for the sacrosanctity of the representative, the Girondins stood too for France—for France, which in these days of imperfect communications slumbered, politically unconscious, and could not overlook its representatives, for France, the abstract, against Paris, the embarrassingly actual, which was exhibiting a disquieting tendency to direct, if not to supersede, the representatives of the people. In 1792 and 1793, if the struggle was to be between Paris and France, the result could not be in doubt. In 1848 and again in 1871 the issue was to be joined again, and France was to defeat Paris; for the electric telegraph and the railway were to modify profoundly the balance of power within France. But the electric telegraph and the steam engine with all they meant to the revolutionary idea lay beyond the horizon of 1793; the hour of France was not yet.

Insisting thus upon the sovereignty of France, the Girondins stood, it is true, for the whole against its part; on their side, they felt, were ethics and logic, every system of both. Unhappily, against them were facts. The Girondins were for what could not be against what was: for what was remote against what was at their doors, the Commune of Paris, embarrassingly ready to guillotine them if need be. In Condorcet's project for the Constitution of 1793 the Revisory National Convention was to sit at least fifty leagues from Paris; Condorcet had learnt his lesson.

And so the conflict of temperamental and intellectual ideals between the groups we call Gironde and Mountain narrowed down to the issue of the sovereignty disputed between France and Paris. This was its secondary form, the shape in which it clothed itself upon the material plane. But it would be a mistake to represent the struggle as either primarily or essentially this.

Jacobinism, the practice of the Mountain, was naturally in direct contrast with Girondin theory. It was an instinct, a reaction to circumstance rather than a creed, and it was seldom that it enunciated anything like a general theory, such as that suggested by the Jacobin manifesto of April 5th, 1793 (signed " Marat, president "), " *Paris doit être le quartier-général de la Révolution.*" " Paris must be the military headquarters of the Revolution." The Jacobin practice could hardly be better epitomised : for it was essentially a product of wartime. Jacobinism was essentially the instinctive reaction of a half practical, half fanatic type of mind to special circumstance, the circumstance of war. But it has some roots a little deeper in the past. Like the Girondins, the Jacobins, too, derive in part from the men of 1789. The men of 1789 had believed passionately that their principles were not only life-giving but true, and as such must command the assent first of France and then of civilisation. They found with dismay that even France refused to be converted and fell apart into factions and civil war. In face of these facts the more academic and less fanatic of the Idealogues evolved the Girondin creed, which, by claiming its due share of power for all France with all its shades of recalcitrant opinion, tacitly admitted that the principles of 1789 were not infallible. Whereas, faced by the same facts, the more fanatic refused to confess that the principles were false and concluded instead that those who opposed the principles were not only obtuse but wicked. " The people," as we shall see in a moment, came to mean those who agreed with the Jacobins, for " virtue is always in a minority."

The Jacobin machinery adapted itself to the Jacobin theory. All over France the affiliated Jacobin societies debated the burning problems of the moment : the mother society of Paris received and collated their conclusions. These decisions became the policy of the Mountain in the Convention ; any deputy who did not support them there was liable to be shouted down, and after the proscription of the Gironde the popular societies altogether controlled the Rump which remained. They had taken an open eye for their device. " The popular societies have always made it their task to supervise the work of the official authorities and of the Government itself. It is this supervision which is the essence of liberty . . . an open eye (l'œil ouvert) fixed on the repositories of power."[1] That is the true spirit of the Terror.

They practised in fact direct control of the people over its representatives. The people, or that minority of the people which was " the people in revolution "— and we shall see in a moment the strange significance of that recurrent phrase—delegated none of its powers. There was no sacrosanctity for its representatives. The electoral assembly of Paris had demanded " comme principe " on September 9th, 1792, that no decree should become law until it had been approved by the people in its primary electoral assemblies. But by 1793 the Jacobins had been driven to establish—in the interests not of the people but " of the people in revolution "—

[1] Moniteur, Jacobins, 16th Oct., 1794.

an even more effective control. The representative had
become the delegate.

The instinctive practice of the Jacobins had in fact
anticipated much modern theory. For the left-wing
movements of to-day maintain increasingly that one
man cannot " represent " a number of others.[1] The
intermittent movement in the trade unionism of to-day
to abolish leadership altogether and to substitute direct
control through fully instructed delegates is the same
discontent with traditional democracy breaking out in
another place. Only, there are scarcely any conditions
under which it is practicable to reduce the representative
to a mere delegate acting under instructions. Normally
mere delegation is impossible, if only because the
opportunities for action pass while the delegate passively
awaits instruction. The singular achievement of the
Jacobins was that the clubs did in fact constitute a
machine which did for a little while reduce the Convention to a delegation. Even while the Committee of
Public Safety terrorised the Convention the mainspring
of the Committee of Public Safety was in the Jacobin
societies.

This practice of direct control of the representatives,
which was the essence of Jacobinism, is the ultimate
cause of two of the most interesting and perplexing
features of these central years. The Terror was established in the name of " the people." But in fact the
people of France lay helpless in the clutches of an
extravagantly small minority. And this minority continually diminished. Everywhere the Jacobin societies
" purified " themselves by sweeping expulsions of their
members. Large numbers by themselves were held to
convict a society of " impurity." " Virtue is always

[1] See, for example, G. D. H. Cole : *Social Theory*, cap. VI.

in a minority," said Robespierre. And it is perhaps
only by being in a minority that " the people " can
retain a grip upon its representatives, can efficiently
" supervise." For supervision demands energy and
attention. Moreover, once " the people " is in power
it must encounter the temptation of all privileged bodies,
the temptation to diminish continually the numbers of
the privileged. Direct democracy can only be exercised
by the few. It is democracy, but it is oligarchy too.
" Virtue is always in a minority," said Robespierre ;
and he had something of this sort in his mind.

The tyrants themselves were conscious that their
tyranny needed justification. And this sense is represented by their habitual use of the words, " the people
in Revolution." For the " people in Revolution " is not
" the People." The words " in Revolution " have the
same implication as the phrase " *Revolutionary* government." *Revolutionary* government, as we shall see,
meant an improvised system which, though unconstitu-
tional, is justified by emergency. And so acts done by
" the people *in Revolution* " may be illegal or immoral
or the usurpation of a minority, but they are justified
by emergency. *Salus populi suprema lex* : such is the
motto both of Revolutionary Government and of the
People in Revolution. The People in Revolution is the
people, as it were, in inverted commas. It may be a
minority, but it is a minority which, to meet a national
emergency, had inevitably to seize power. " The people "
is helpless, remote, a political abstraction. " The people
in revolution " must usurp its authority if France and
the Revolution are to be saved.

Again : Jacobinism had no leaders. Perhaps France
before 1799 could in any case not have produced what we
call great men. But in a special sense these central years

had no leaders. How could there be leaders ? Leaders
and direct democracy : these could not co-exist. The
quality of the men whom these years fling up, and pre-
eminently of Robespierre, is not leadership, but acute
instinct for what the moment permits. Indeed the most
arresting characteristic of Robespierre is precisely his
mediocrity. He so clearly had none of the qualities of
leadership. How can this man have been a leader ?
is a question that has been often asked. And the answer
is that he was not a leader. At best he interpreted to
" the people in revolution " its own will. The terrible
power which he seemed to wield was the power of the
people in revolution ; it might abandon him on the
morrow, but while he remained its direct agent he was
irresistible. And what was destroyed in Thermidor was
not Robespierre, who was a shadow, nor the Commune
of Paris, which was a machine, but Jacobinism, direct
democracy.

There are plenty of traces that the men of the Terror
themselves were conscious that they were instruments,
irresistibly impelled by forces for ever beyond their
control, marionettes who could live only until their
string was cut. " I am not the champion of the people,"
said Robespierre ; " I have never claimed so arrogant
a title. I am of the people. I have never been more
than that. I despise anyone who has pretentions to be
more." Again, " I had orders." That is the solitary
defence of Fouquier Tinville of the Revolutionary
Tribunal, reiterated at each new charge when at last
he himself stands before his judges. " I was an axe "
(wielded by something greater than myself), pleads
another Terrorist. And the defence was sound. Neither
Robespierre nor Tinville nor any other Jacobin stands
ever by himself. All are instruments. Jacobinism, the

Terror, had no captains; "a dictatorship without a dictator," said the Jacobins themselves.[1]

Danton alone perhaps attempted to lead; in spite of direct democracy to impose his own will. And Danton was guillotined *as a traitor to the people*. Is it possible that the sombre lethargy into which he subsided during his last days, the strange apathy which would not even struggle against his approaching fate, was due to a bewildering suspicion that after all the charge against him was true? For he was indeed a traitor—to Jacobinism; not, that is, to the People—for the People was non-existent—but to " the People in Revolution."

Direct democracy, the tyranny of the minority, this was the soul of Jacobinism. And naturally it stamped itself ineffaceably upon its machinery—Revolutionary Government.

It is better to think of these central years of the Revolution, August, 1792, to July, 1794, not as the period of " the Terror " (which is, at the best, a loose designation, and carries a false implication), but as the period of Revolutionary Government. Revolutionary Government was an improvisation in face of the threat of the armies of the first coalition from without, and the threat, imaginary to some extent, of the traitor-aristocrats from within. There can be no doubt that the threat of a foreign intervention in alliance with the Emigrés played an incalculable part in forcing France to accept the Revolutionary Government of Paris. Like the foreign intervention with the Russian Revolution, it fused, or temporarily quieted, what were really discordant elements. For while the peril lasted the nation was bound to tolerate any *de facto* government which could

[1] See for a brilliant analysis of Jacobinism, Cochin : *La Crise de l'histoire révolutionnaire.*

direct and energise the national defence. It was not until *after* the danger had passed that the Terror collapsed. Attack from without must always be of the greatest possible service to an energetic national administration. The machinery of the Terror, therefore, was not contrived upon any considered plan; it was flung together in the fever fits of a nation defending itself, it supposed, against two great perils.

The essence, we saw, of the Jacobin system of direct democracy was the clubs. And the first, though perhaps not the most essential, characteristic of revolutionary government is the absorption of the club into the machinery of administration. For it was not enough that the People in Revolution should have its hand upon the legislators; the whole administrative system must be within its grasp.

The decree of 14 Frimaire year II (December 4th, 1793) entrusted the Jacobin societies all over France with the election and supervision of municipal functionaries. But the decree was only recognising a right which had here and there already been assumed.[1]

The *représentants en mission*, those members of the Convention despatched after the proscription of the Gironde to restore the control of the central authority over the provinces, worked usually hand-in-glove with the local Jacobin clubs; which thus were admitted to a share in local administration. Transformed into " popular societies," the Jacobin clubs were treated by the *représentants en mission* as part of the actual machinery of government. We shall have to consider the *représentants en mission* later.

In touch, too, with the clubs were the *comités révolutionnaires*, committees of twelve set up all over the

[1] *E.g.*, The Jacobins of Arles in September, 1793 (Aulard, 349.)

country (21st March, 1793) to hunt out and punish spies
of all degrees and types ; *comités de surveillance* they had
been even more suggestively called, and they exercised,
and often abused, very terrible powers.

Thus through the clubs the people in revolution laid
hold upon the administration of France. But this entry
of the club into the machinery of administration is
perhaps not the most distinctive feature of revolutionary
government. At any rate, to a contemporary, " Revolutionary Government " would have had a different and
very definite connotation. By revolutionary government a Parisian of 1793 would have understood that
improvised system of government which as a war-time
expedient had provisionally neglected Article XVI of
the Declaration of Rights of 1789. Article XVI had
declared that a society in which the powers (legislative
and executive) are not separate has no constitution.
We have come across this curious dogma of the separation of powers already. We saw that this mistrust
inherited from the *ancien régime* was gospel with the
men of 1789 and that on this rock were wrecked Mirabeau's schemes for a strong responsible ministry. At any
cost, all good revolutionaries believed, members of the
legislative must not be ministers. This paralysing creed
had little difficulty in surviving the already chaotic
constitution of 1791, but with war and the growing need
for effective government the inexorable logic of facts
proved it more and more an anachronism. The
reluctance of the Revolution to deny this article of the
primitive revolutionary creed is pathetically obvious in
the tentative and surreptitious manner in which it went
about the business. Thus on August 10th, 1792, the
king's government had come to an end and the legislative assembly elected a *Conseil Exécutif Provisoire*

(Provisional Executive Council) of six ministers, not members of the assembly itself. The " powers " were still " separate," but it was tacitly understood that the ministry should be responsible to the assembly, and from September, 1792, the Convention issued direct orders to it. It was a separate but responsible executive. On January 3rd, 1793, the Revolution took the next hesitating step towards fusion. The Convention appointed a *Comité de Défense Générale* (Committee of General Defence) from among its members, to collaborate with the Council of Ministers. Thus, although the members of the Convention were not theoretically executive ministers, they were to collaborate with, and supervise, them, and it was clearly only a question of time until this, or some later committee of members, should reduce to mere secretaries the original Council of Ministers and so in practice make the legislature and the executive one. The *Comité de Défense Générale* was too large and too public and it was discredited by the defeats of Aix-la-Chapelle and Neerwinden.

On March 25th, 1793, it was expanded and its control over the executive council more precisely defined. And two of its members were always to be present in the Convention to reply to questions ; another half-hearted step towards assumption of executive power by the legislative. But the *Comité Générale* could not be expected to survive the treason of Dumouriez. And the necessity of finally combining legislature and executive was becoming clearer every day. " We cannot hide it from ourselves," said Danton, " ministers are needed whose necessary and habitual contact with you will assure the uniformity and execution of the measures you have contrived for the public safety."

On April 6th, 1793, came the inevitable final steps.

The Committee of Public Safety (*Comité de Salut Public*) created then consisted of sixteen members of the Convention. And this committee did actually reduce the ministers of the *Conseil Exécutif Provisoire* to the position of its secretaries. In practice then there is at last (though not even now, observe, in theory) complete fusion of the executive and legislature. And to a contemporary this fusion would have been the meaning of revolutionary government.

And clearly this fusion was pretty directly due to the practice of direct democracy. The people in revolution had achieved control of the legislature. Is it not to control the executive too ? What is more natural than that for this purpose the two spheres of government should gradually coalesce, like clay beneath the hand of the new potter ? That is why the administration and the legislature unite ; because the legislature is already in " the people's " grasp. Direct democracy is the essence of Jacobinism and revolutionary government is its embodiment.

Revolutionary government is thus essentially *provisional*. " The government of France is revolutionary till the peace," said the decree of October 10th, 1793 ; that is, until conditions are once more normal it suspends constitutional government and the Constitution of 1793 (voted June 24th). " Revolutionary ! " The word may almost be taken as meaning " justified by abnormal circumstances." This, we saw, was the implication of the phrase " the People in Revolution." This is the implication, too, of the *Revolutionary* tribunal, instituted on March 10th, 1793, to expedite justice against the counter-revolutionaries.

Direct democracy is the essence of Jacobinism. These central years have other features and striking ones, but

this was their fundamental characteristic. The others,
in a greater or less degree, were accidental. The
massacres themselves, which have given these years
their name, were accidental. They were a war-time
spy-fever ; in our own way we have been through the
fit ourselves, and we know that it comes from fright.
The Terror was due to terror. There has been a literary
propaganda of the Terror ; the death of rich and
aristocratic persons struck, and strikes, the imagination.
But in point of fact the executions and imprisonments
of the Revolution, though it was then on the verge of
destruction by enemies without and within, never
reached the ferocity of those of the Conservative
Government of 1871 when it had already triumphed
unassailably over all its foes. But it was the poor
and the unknown who (once more) were martyred
in 1871, and literature has had no concern with their
sufferings.

On the ninth of Thermidor, as we said, it was not
Robespierre who fell, but a system. The essential
Revolution beneath a score of distracting influences
and cross-currents was labouring to achieve Equality
and Order. In the fever fit of its central years it did in
fact instinctively rather than intentionally evolve a
short-lived system of direct democracy ; and this it was
which perished on that July afternoon when Robespierre,
its shadow, was hauled half-dying on to the platform
of the guillotine. We shall find the ghost of the
dead system re-appearing, a little half-hearted, in the
Revolution of 1848, only to be driven underground again
(together with the new revolutionary idea which fathered
it then) by the horrified heirs of the orthodox tradition
of the Revolution of 1789 ; and it will rise transiently
to haunt Paris again for a little while in 1871.

The transient experiment with direct democracy was
both the principal achievement and the explanation of
the Terror ; this cannot be too often repeated, for it is
of fundamental importance. But the Terror had naturally other distinctive characteristics which were all, we
said, in a greater or less degree accidental ; not cause
but effect, that is, of the circumstances of the time (the
national resistance to invasion). But of these accidental
characteristics there is one which we ought to examine
a little more closely. What was the relation of this
experiment in direct democracy to (what we now call)
Socialism ? For " Socialism " (it is of course an
anachronism to use the word " Socialism " at any rate
before 1848) is sooner or later to play its part in the
history of the revolutionary idea. But when ? Was
there anything that can be called Socialism during the
Terror ?

It has been suggested that Robespierre was a Socialist.
The view has some plausibility, for during the strange
pullulation of the Socialist idea during the July monarchy
Robespierre's project for a Declaration of Rights of
April, 1793, was many times reprinted, as a sort of
Charter of Socialism ; and Robespierre himself was
looked back upon as the father and archetype of
Socialists. And in spite of the fact that its author took
the precaution of introducing it by the assertions that
" Equality of wealth is a chimera " and " It is much
more important to make poverty honourable than to
proscribe riches " (which he meant no doubt for a
disavowal of Socialism, albeit Socialism, needless to say,
has never aimed at " equality of wealth "), yet there
certainly is about that once celebrated declaration a
certain Socialist flavour. ". . . . The right of property
like all other rights is bounded by the obligation of

respecting the rights of others. It cannot be allowed
to prejudice the safety, the liberty, the existence or the
property of our fellows. Any commerce which violates
this principle is essentially illicit and immoral." He
suggests, further, exemption from taxation of those whose
incomes are not above the subsistence-level, and again
" It is the duty of society to provide for the subsistence
of all its members, whether by furnishing them with
employment or by guaranteeing the means of existence
to those who are unable to work."[1]

Such was the " Socialist " declaration of Robespierre.
But the fact is that neither Robespierre nor the Jacobins
who approved his Declaration were Socialist. The truth
is that the Girondin project for the Constitution of 1793
was so democratic that, in order to depopularise it, and
as a move in the political struggle, Robespierre and the
Jacobins had to go one better by avowing themselves
Socialists, partisans of the *loi agraire* they had just
ridiculed as a " phantom invented by rogues to frighten
imbeciles." The declaration was a party move intended
" to dish the Girondins " as Disraeli's Reform Act
" dished the Whigs " in 1867 : M. Aulard has made
this clear.[2] That it was no more than this, and not part
of a sinister Socialist plot engineered by " world-
revolutionaries," is sufficiently proved by the fact that
when, scarcely more than a month later, the Girondins
were crushed and the Jacobins were masters of the
situation, they did in fact insert into their Declaration
of Rights no single one of the articles contained in the
project of Robespierre, nor did Robespierre ever propose
them again. None the less (as Victorien Sardou not

[1] The speech (in translation) will be found in Postgate : *Revolution from* 1789
 to 1906, p. 43.
[2] *Op. cit.*, pp. 448 foll.

unhumorously observed) a century after his death
Robespierre still had his dupes. The only serious proposal
of any sort of Socialist measures came from Hébert and
Chaumette, who had suggested that the Revolution
might assume control of raw material and workshops,
and under whose influence the Commune threatened
Socialist tendencies. But Hébert and Chaumette were
guillotined as "factious," and both had been abandoned
by their following before their death.

So much for the declaration which earned Robespierre
his prestige among the Socialists of the eighteen-forties.
But did direct democracy, apart from this, commit
itself to anything that can be called Socialist legislation?
Socialism is a word which has unfortunately developed
a dangerous variety of implication. If we are to understand it inexactly (as it is very often understood) to
cover any measure of which (what we call) Socialists
might be expected to approve, the answer to our question
requires a little investigation. For the Terror, we have
seen, was essentially empirical, and as such inconsistent;
and it legislated inconsistently too. And here it will be
convenient to defer for a moment a final answer to the
question: Was the Terror, in this inexact sense,
Socialist? For in the next section I shall try to consider
the Terror, no longer as a phenomenon by itself (for as
such it can never be completely intelligible), but,
incidentally, as a stage in the gradual achievement of
the aims with which the Revolution set out: and the
realisation of one of these aims, equality (or the abolition
of feudal privilege), implied legislation of a kind which
might be called Socialist in this looser sense: so that
the consideration of that part of this legislation which
falls in the period of the Terror will serve to answer
in further detail our question: Was the Terror in the

inexact sense Socialist ?—and we may for the moment postpone it.

But it is worth while to point out at this stage that, whether this anti-feudal legislation of the Revolution and the Terror can reasonably be labelled " Socialist " or not, it was not at least a meaningless product of a merely malevolent and subterranean agitation by a handful of conspirators.[1] On the contrary, it was the constant and deliberate aim of the majority of Frenchmen, of that great aggregate of wills which we call the Revolution ; and once achieved it has time after time enlisted the majority of Frenchmen in its defence and become at last, thanks mainly to the peasants, perhaps the most central and conservative force in modern France. But, even without considering for the moment the contribution of the Terror to the destruction of feudalism (which was very far from being completed on August 4th, 1789,[2] its so-called St. Bartholomew), we shall see reason to conclude that the Convention's decree of March 18th, 1793, was in fact the *credo* of the Revolution. " The National Convention decrees the death penalty against any person who proposes a *loi agraire,* or any other law subversive of property, whether landed or commercial or industrial."[3] The Revolution always admitted unrestricted private property, even if it sometimes proposed to transfer it from the rich to the poor. Babœuf, the communist, was imprisoned by the Terror and executed by the Directory, and his theories are of no more than negative importance to the Revolutionary

---

[1] As is suggested by, *e.g.*, Mrs. Webster: *The French Revolution: a Study in Democracy.*

[2] V. infra, p. 76.

[3] *La Convention nationale décrète la peine de mort contre quiconque proposera une loi agraire ou tout autre subversive des propriétés territoriales, commerciales et industrielles.*

idea until 1828, when they were revived by Buonarotti's *Histoire de la Conspiration de Babœuf.*

For the Socialist movement which was to graft itself upon the Revolutionary idea between the years 1830 and 1848 was mostly collectivist and essentially an appeal to the industrial workers. And consequently those whose creed it is that all Revolution is the mysterious work of one constant world-conspiracy are naturally inclined to represent both the Terror and the Revolution of 1789 as similarly a movement of the masses which made for the collectivist idea. But both the Terror, and the whole Revolution of 1789, of which it is the quintessence, were essentially individualist and essentially middle class.

In this connection the law of June 14th, 1791 (*loi le Chapelier*) is instructive and has not received the attention it deserves. It is designed to prevent associations of workmen to raise wages ; the work of a middle class assembly of masters.[1] It forbids citizens of the same status or profession to organise themselves " in their alleged common interest," or to threaten " any who are contented with lower pay." " All large meetings of artisans, workers and journeymen . . . are to be considered seditious and punished as such." *This law was never repealed, even by the Mountain, during the Terror.* Indeed the Committee of Public Safety was even more apprehensive than the Legislative Assembly of industrial agitation. And when organising the Arm factories it ordained that workers from different manufactories might only communicate through a third party or by permission of their respective managements. And in any case they were not to meet together to

---

[1] The principal contents of the *loi le Chapelier* will be found (translated) in Postgate : *Revolution from* 1789 *to* 1906, p. 37.

represent their grievances. The artisan was the principal victim of the Revolution, which did so much for the peasant.

It is true that the progressive income tax suggested in Robespierre's speech of April 24th, 1793, took shape finally, after several experiments, on September 3rd of that year, as a tax which actually reached 100 per cent. on incomes which only just exceeded what may be called the average middle class standard ; but it is not at all clear to what extent this tax was really applied, or, given the rapid fall of the value of money and the impossibility of elaborate administrative machinery, was applicable.

Indeed, although it was the legislation of the Terror that consummated all that the Revolution did for the poor, the power of the Terror was not primarily founded upon the *sans-culotte* masses of Paris : " the people in Revolution " was never the people, even of Paris. It is true that the decree of September 9th, 1793, allowed 40 sous a day to the poor citizens who attended assemblies of their sections ; but although direct democracy was prepared to go thus far to propitiate them, that close corporation never dreamed of identifying itself wholly with the *sans-culottes*. Both Gironde and Mountain were altogether middle class parties, and the Convention contained perhaps no member of the proletariat.

We have so far been considering the Terror, the expression of Jacobinism, as a solitary phenomenon. And naturally it can only be completely understood when viewed as part of a whole. By itself it is the transient embodiment of an almost mystical political principle. But it does not stand by itself.

CHAPTER IV

THE ACHIEVEMENT OF THE REVOLUTION

AFTER the collapse of direct democracy on the 9th Thermidor, 1794, France passed into a phase of suspended animation. As we shall see, of the two principal aims with which, long before 1789, the Revolution had originated, by 1794 one was already accomplished and the other had begun in 1792 to move tentatively towards completion. To guarantee and perpetuate the one conquest, and to complete the other, France awaited the strong hand. Meanwhile the Revolution progressed no further : it waited. The key of the years between Thermidor and Brumaire, the death of Robespierre and the coming of Buonaparte, is—expectation. We recapture that pervading uneasy anticipation everywhere in the history of these years : in their manners and morals, the *bals des victimes* and the *mode grecque* (for levity in a society goes almost always with impermanence) : in the memoirs of the time : in all the policy of the Directory, clinging to power like the drowning to a floating spar and saddling the country therefore abroad with war at any price to distract the army, and at home with the " see-saw " of *coup d'états* alternately against left and right. Everywhere it was felt that, sooner rather than later, either the Revolution and its achievements must be destroyed or else they must be consolidated and guaranteed : sooner or later uncertainty must end. Either the *émigrés*, or —— ? Perhaps the only positive achievement of the years of the Directory was more clearly every month to answer that unspoken question. The answer was—Napoleon ; for the army could not permanently be distracted.

For us, then, concerned with the revolutionary idea, the period of the Directory is essentially an interim ; and its history the history of a stop-gap, even at the time recognised more and more consciously as such. And therefore it matters little that the Directory was a qualified return to the principle of middle class electoral privilege which had collapsed in 1792. In the essentials of the aims of the Revolution, as we shall see in a moment, the Directory scarcely moved either back or forward ; it marked time. Indeed, it could not move. Its constitution, in the first place, was based upon one principle only, and a negative one at that—no more Robespierre—and lasting constitutions cannot be built upon negative principles alone. It " organised conflict " ; that is to say, it provided no constitutional method for resolving the inevitable disputes between the twofold legislature and the executive of five Directors. And dispute was inevitable, for the Directory had only one policy—to cling to power. The directors were regicides, and they had deserted their colleagues of the Terror, and, once out of power, they must fall to the vengeance of either Royalist or Jacobin. It was only a choice between the rope and the guillotine. Hence their domestic policy is a mere see-saw of *coup d'états* against whichever of their avengers at the moment were most threatening, the party of the rope or the party of the guillotine. And their foreign policy was as simple—to keep the army busy. But to keep the army busy meant, under the circumstances, to keep it powerful. And a powerful army meant Cæsar.

What was the relation of Cæsar to the Revolution ? The answer of Bonaparte himself to this question was unequivocal. He said, " I am the Revolution." What right had he to that huge claim ? Or, in other words, what had been the essential tendencies and achievements of the Revolution hitherto, and did the Empire guarantee them or betray ? Further, in tracing the gradual achievement of these aims we shall discover characteristics in the various stages of the Revolution which were not to be detected when we considered those stages by themselves. The Terror, for example, has hitherto appeared to us the fever fit of the Revolution, and we have seen that the Terror was the embodiment of a theory which died with it : but we shall see now that the Terror was also, curiously enough, the point at which the Revolution began to revert to tradition.

The Revolution, we have seen, was at its outset a movement for order and a movement for equality, and we must trace separately the effort to accomplish each of these aims if we are to have any true or even clear conception of the course and achievement of the Revolution. And, what is more, within a whole so infinitely complex as this Revolution merely to isolate a set of phenomena in this way may in itself be a considerable assistance.

The desire for order was perhaps the most fundamental of the motives which originated the Revolution, because it was, as we have seen, the motive which most closely affected the middle classes who were the Revolution's authors. Now in 1789 the middle classes wanted order not in one department only but all through the State ; but order rests upon local administration, and if we

examine briefly the chief features of the local administration of France, and the constant changes it underwent
from the day of the *paroisse* of the *ancien régime* to that
of the *commune* of the first Empire we shall be most
likely to reach a fair estimate of the reality of the
Revolution's achievement in the matter of order.

Now administration under the *ancien régime* was a
centralisation, but it was a corrupt and chaotic centralisation. Administration passed with maddening
inefficiency and delays along a chain extending from the
conseil du roi and the *contrôleur général* through the
intendant and the *subdélégué* to the humblest *collecteurs*
or *syndics* of the *paroisse*. The *paroisse* whose church
had had the tiles blown from its roof in a gale must
wait for permission from the *conseil du roi* to put them
back. No wonder that the typical *paroisse* of the
ancien régime was, in Turgot's words, " a collection of
huts, and of inhabitants as passive as their huts." And
it was the same with the towns. " We have never
resisted your wishes, my lord," write municipal officers
to their *intendant*. For the centralisation of the *ancien
régime* was numbing without being efficient.

In 1790 the Idealogues of the Constituent Assembly,
luxuriating in their strange belief in man's infinite
perfectibility and the beautiful virtue of his " natural
state," had arrived in consequence at their pathetic
determination to break altogether with the fettering
traditions of the past. They concluded accordingly
that if the people of France, utterly untrained in self
administration, were altogether freed from control, all
would be for the best in a world that Rousseau would
have smiled on. Accordingly they sub-divided the
departments and districts into which they had just
partitioned France into close on forty thousand all but

autonomous *communes*. Not only every town and village
but every huddle of cottages was to have its own separate
administration. And naturally the vast majority of the
communes failed entirely to discover among themselves
even moderately efficient administration. Thanks to the
Idealogues the pendulum had swung too far. This was
decentralisation run to anarchy, an anarchy more
disastrous even than the chaos of the *ancien régime* ; a
whirling dust storm whose particles were infinitely
minute.

When war had come and France was threatened with
invasion, the Convention, in the effort to rouse and
organise the national defence, inevitably felt the need
of central control. Hence the *représentants en mission*.
These were members of the Convention itself, sent out
by it with authority (decree of March 9th, 1793), " . . . to
take all measures which they may think necessary to
re-establish order." This of March, 1793, was not the
first appearance of *représentants en mission* ; indeed, as
long ago as 22nd June, 1791, during the suspension of
the king's authority after the flight to Varennes, the
Constituent Assembly had despatched some of its
members to the frontier ; but this decree of 9th March,
1793, which authorised the mission of eighty-two representatives, was the first use on a large scale of an
expedient which was to develop further still. For, like
all the machinery of revolutionary government, it was
an expedient. The use of *représentants en mission* was
in fact a return to centralisation ; but it was a surreptitious return. No doubt the Convention's hesitation
to abolish the decentralisation of the Constitution of
1791 openly and at one blow came partly from the
familiar superstition of the " separation of the powers "
—for the system of *représentants en mission* meant an

unmistakable fusion of legislature and executive—and
partly too from the very nature of revolutionary government, whose most far-reaching provisions as we have
seen came gradually and as provisional expedients rather
than calculated legislation; but surely it was due partly,
too, to a very intelligible reluctance to avow openly, as it
were, the bankruptcy of the golden visions of 1789. We
have seen that this reluctance was one of the fundamental
sources of the Jacobin temper, which concluded not that
the principles of 1789 were false, but that their opponents
were immoral persons and enemies of " the people." And
we shall find the same reluctance even more conspicuous
in the decorous veiling of the change of the official
attitude to military aggression at the end of 1792.

By a later decree the *représentants en mission* were
replaced by the *agents nationaux*, permanent agents with
limited powers, much less independent than the *représentants*, some of whom had completely disregarded their
instructions. This was centralisation gone a step further.
The Terror had reverted unmistakably to centralisation ;
but it had never explicitly acknowledged the reversion.

Immediately after Thermidor, in a natural but
transient reaction from anything that smacked of the
Terror, the Convention returned a little way towards
decentralisation ; but when it was time to patch together
the Directorial Constitution of the year III, the logic of
necessity had proved too strong, and the Directory,
though less confidently than the Convention, continued
the retreat towards the centralising traditions of the
ancien régime. Like its legislative system the administrative system of the Directory was a compromise, like the
legislative system it was Girondin in design, and like the
legislative system it was stamped with every characteristic of impermanence. In each department was to be an

elected " central administration " of five, but the Directory itself could override the decisions of this body and cashier its members. It attached also to the activities of the " central administration " of each department a *commissaire* chosen from among the local inhabitants but directly under its own orders. The " districts " of 1790 were abolished : there was to be no administrative body intermediate between the department and the municipalities, *communes* as they had been called. But many of the country *communes* had been so small that they had never become organic and some of the town communes so large that they had never been safe. Hence the *canton* ; a new unit which was an aggregation of several *communes*, where the population was under 5,000, or alternatively a subdivision of those in which it was over 100,000. These municipal administrations were under the direct control of the departmental, and to each of them too was attached the *commissaire* with his watching brief.

This was centralisation of a sort, it is true ; a long retreat from the position of 1790 ; but for all that it was a compromise. For in such a system as this the impulse must come from the local unit. It is true that the central authority retained the right of checking the impulse and that when there was conflict between them the local unit almost always gave way : but the point is that, subject to whatever restraints and limitations, the initiative came not from above but from below. Not from above, as it came, incoherently enough, with the *représentants en mission* of the Terror. Not from above, as it was to come, uninterrupted and with terrific force, in the system of Napoleon. The forms at any rate of administration under the Directory implied a less effective centralisation than those of the Terror. It is a

striking testimony to that submissive instinct in France
which we have to notice so often that in practice the
habit of perpetual reference to Paris was hardening all
through these years 1794-1799. So M. Aulard concludes
from the surviving correspondence of the Directorial
commissaires which was both " more rapid and more
regular than that of the *agents nationaux* or the *représentants en mission.*"

In this matter of administration the Revolution, then,
was moving by fits and starts, but unmistakably, back
to the centralisation of the *ancien régime*. What of
Napoleon ? Napoleon completed that movement. We
may say of him indifferently that he " organised the
ancien régime " or that he consolidated the Revolution :
for the two processes were identical. The Empire preserved the departments ; but in the interests of despotism
and centralisation it substituted for the *cantons* of the
Directory, which had been large enough to threaten to
become organic, the *arrondissements communaux*, which
were once more small enough to be impotent : and as a
matter of fact, still in the interests of centralisation,
France is divided into these same *communes* to-day. For
centralisation is in the blood of Frenchmen ; and
Frenchmen must be administered even if they are not
governed. Over each of these districts was placed a
prefect, and, at his orders, in each *arrondissement* a sub-
prefect. And the authority of *préfet* and *sous-préfet* was
altogether unimpaired by the quite negligible powers of
the *conseils généraux* (in the department) and of the
conseils d'arrondissement, which amounted to very little
more than the right of apportioning direct taxation
(during their sessions of a fortnight every year). For the
impulse came no longer from below : and it was not now
the representative of the central authority who was

concerned, like the Directory's *commissaire*, to observe
or check that impulse : irresistibly now the impulse
descended from above, and it was for the local unit with
what derisive shreds of opportunity were left to it to
do what it could to watch and placate its master. And
what were these *préfets* and *sous-préfets* if not the
intendants and the *subdelégués* of the *ancien régime* risen
from the dead ? Risen from the dead, but with this one
inestimable difference : that, whereas whole-hearted
centralisation had France in its clutches once again, and
once again authority passed down an unbroken chain
from its source, the Emperor, through *préfet* and *sous-
préfet* to the impotent, inorganic *arrondissements communaux*, yet this was organised despotism in place of
chaotic despotism, order where there had been disorder,
instead of impotence, strength.

Napoleon had organised the *ancien régime.* " The
Revolution ? " he had said, " I am the Revolution " ;
and it was true, for in that achievement he was the
Revolution. In him and through him the Revolution
had reached its first great goal—Order, and so lastingly
had that aim been attained, so consonantly with the
genius of France, that to this day, after all its changes
of government, save for a few most trifling modifications,
France continues to be administered by Napoleon. For
Frenchmen " liberty " remains a catchword, signifying
little—unlike Englishmen, they desire government more
than freedom. Order : this was the prime aim of the
Revolution, and towards this, as we have seen, it had
struggled unceasingly, beneath the distracting cross-
currents of that attempt of the early Idealogues to
cut loose altogether from the traditions of the past ;
and this, with the Constitution of the year VIII, it
had achieved. This achievement alone gives to the

Revolution justification and a meaning. This achievement alone makes it impossible to conceive the Revolution philosophically, for example, as certain writers have
tried to depict it[1]—as the blindly destructive assault on
civilisation of secret societies, purposeless as a child
who pulls the wings from a fly.

The Revolution had been a movement to introduce
order and equality. And these were the two great changes
it was to effect. But there was one possession upon which
perhaps Frenchmen set as much store as even upon order
or equality—*la dictature de l'Europe*,[2] a glorious foreign
policy. And it is important to remember that the
revolutionary movement dates not from the years when
le roi soleil was spending the blood and treasure of
France in his glorious but not very profitable raids on
Europe but from the time when Louis XV was first
bamboozled and then defeated by Frederic the Great.
Frenchmen had applauded the victories of Frederic even
over the armies of France, not only because he was an
enlightened despot, but because he was a military hero
too. And the attitude of France to glory makes a very
striking illustration of this central tendency of the
Revolution to which I have drawn attention, this fundamental tendency—once past that attempted cleavage of
the men of 1789—to be carried helplessly back towards
the traditions of the old *régime*. We have just seen that
tendency conspicuously in operation in the matter of the
achievement of order. And before I go on to sketch the

[1] *E.g.*, Mrs. Webster : *The French Revolution : a Study in Democracy.* It may be
noted, too, that since the gradual realisation of the aims of the Revolution
of 1789 went on (as we shall see again) up to and after the coming of
Bonaparte, any sketch of the Revolution which stops short, as does
Mrs. Webster's, with the fall of Robespierre must be ultimately untrue.

[2] " *Les biens auxquels les Français attachaient le plus de prix—l'égalité civile
et la dictature de l'Europe.*"   Bourgeois. *Manuel historique de politique
étrangère*, ii. 117.

second great effort of the Revolution, the effort to establish equality, it will be instructive to see briefly how here, too, in foreign policy, the same broad principles are at work and how its history in the years between 1789 and 1799 has essentially the same characteristics : a short-lived effort to break loose from tradition, followed by a steady, and in this case uninterrupted, reversion to the deep-seated instincts of the past.

La dictature de l'Europe, glory ; such had been the ambition of the rulers of France under the old order ; and aggression had been their means to this end. An aggressive foreign policy was the tradition of the *ancien régime*, and the people had been proud of the tradition. Indeed, even the philosophers were Frenchmen before they were philosophers. Rousseau had declared that the natural frontiers (the Alps, the Rhine, the sea, and the Pyrenees) must, as the work of nature itself, be conquered or maintained. And Raynal, though he admitted that Richelieu was a " bloody murderer," reminded his readers that for all that he deserved their admiration, for he was the first to teach France her true position in Europe.

Aggression was the traditional policy of France, and naturally the Idealogues, setting out gloriously to build a new world in 1789, determined to have no more of it. The Idealogue alternative can be easily summed up : for their foreign policy was to have no foreign policy ; and it was admirably epitomised in the Constituent Assembly's Declaration of May, 1790 : " France renounces the idea of conquest." Was a completer breach with the past conceivable ? And could any policy have been more inevitably short-lived ?

This profession of pacifism, in face of a Europe about to arm for a partition of France which should rival and

complete the partitions of Poland, was in effect recanted
before the close of 1791. But with that curious reluctance
to acknowledge explicitly the bankruptcy of the golden
visions of the Revolution's dawn—a reluctance which we
have already detected in the Convention's tacit return
to centralisation—the first threats which the Revolution
permitted itself were veiled decorously in the language
of the decree of 1790. It threatened, but it threatened
in the jargon of pacifism. The remarkable self-deception
embodied in the phraseology of the decree of November
29th, 1791, is worth observing. "Tell the foreign powers,"
the king was exhorted, "that we stand faithfully by our
oath to make no conquest ; that we shall respect their
laws and their constitutions, but that ours must be
respected too. Tell them that if the German princes
continue to abet preparations against France, we shall
invade them, not with fire and sword, but with—
liberty . . . ."

The next stage was reached with inexorable ease. The
Revolution could not perhaps have avoided the war
which came with the spring of 1792 : in spite of the
arrière-pensées of many of those who united for very
different reasons in welcoming it, it was in origin
essentially a defensive war. But the cannonade of Valmy
(September 20th, 1792) changed all that. By the 23rd of
October French territory was altogether clear of invaders.
But was the war over ? Many of the volunteers of 1792
thought that it was ; they proposed to disband themselves. But the Convention was already suffering the fate
which inevitably overtakes any *de facto* government
which has improvised an army : it was in mortal terror
of its own creation. The shadow of Cæsar was cast seven
years before him. "The thousands of troops whom we
have under arms," said Roland, "must be packed off

as far as their legs will carry them. Otherwise they would
cut our throats." And so " Has the enemy crossed the
Rhine ? " demands the decree of October 24th. "Has the
enemy crossed the Rhine ? " The generals are to be kept
busy. Observe : the natural frontiers entering history.
But as a matter of fact the Convention need not have
been so apprehensive : it had no need to stimulate the
aggressive passions either of generals or people. A new
force, the awakening sense of nationality, had done the
work for it already. France felt itself for the first time
an organic whole, for the first time a whole in which each
citizen had a stake ; and in the ardour of that new
inspiration it was going out upon a new crusade. The
Convention had but to wait upon events. Its generals
did not linger for instructions. After Valmy, Custine on
the Rhine and Anselme in Nice took the offensive all
but instinctively ; and behind them all France thrilled
with the *élan* of the old instinct for aggression re-expressed
in the new sense of organic nationhood. Valmy (20th
September) is separated from Jemmapes (6th November)
not by six weeks merely. Between them lies all the
difference between the Revolution fighting for its life
and the Revolution embarking, albeit in a new spirit,
upon a war of aggrandisement which might have been
taken bodily out of the reign of Louis XIV. The victory
of the French at Valmy occasioned some surprise in
Europe. But there was no occasion for surprise, for two
centuries met at Valmy ; and it could hardly be won-
dered at that the nineteenth century triumphed over the
eighteenth.

Between Valmy and Jemmapes, on October 24th, as
we saw, the generals were reminded that the Prussians
had not crossed the Rhine. And henceforth the jargon of
the *natural frontiers* is to bulk larger and larger in the

records of the time. For the truth is that behind this
semi-mystic doctrine of the natural frontiers once again
the Revolution was decorously veiling its own apostasy:
or, to speak the language of psychology, we may say that
the Revolution was *rationalising its motives*. The natural
frontiers, that is to say, were the conveniently hypnotic
label with which it sought to persuade itself, and Europe,
that the passage from Valmy to Jemmapes was not a
mere relapse to the traditions of the *ancien régime*. This
mystic phrase " The Natural Frontiers "—with all its
vague implications of Rousseau and natural right—was
a subconscious attempt to keep the wars of 1793 at the
moral level of the declaration of 1790, by suggesting that
they too represented a new principle. France, the suggestion was, had not baldly reverted to the *ancien régime*:
on the contrary she had progressed to a different, but an
equally novel and exalted and revolution-worthy policy.
No doubt there was much self-deception here. But none
the less we must not forget that the revolutionary wars
of aggression did have this of novelty, that the driving
force behind them was the new sense of nationality,
entering for the first time the history of France.

From this point the foreign policy of the Revolution,
with which we have no direct concern, is only a development of the same theme : Merlin de Thionville expressed
the spirit of it when he declared " The Republic must
dictate laws to Europe" (29th Nov., 1794). War, because
the nation desired glory, and after that because un-
occupied generals were likely to be dangerous. And then
Napoleon, and the passion for glory fiercer and more
amply satisfied still.

Here, too, then, Napoleon developed, completed that
same tendency in the Revolution, the tendency to return
on its steps back to the traditions of the old order. Here

too he could claim, "I am the Revolution." And here too, since he did consummately what the later Bourbons tried, but failed to do, he may be said to have organised the *ancien régime*.

As we have seen, the movement for order had been primarily the concern of the middle classes, while the other great discontent in which the Revolution had originated, the movement for equality, had meant much less to the middle classes[1] than to the peasants, for whom equality implied the abolition of feudalism. Had the Revolution abolished feudalism ?

We must be on our guard against a common error. Feudalism was *not* destroyed on the night of August 4th, 1789. It is true that the sentimentalists of that time, and their successors, hailed August 4th as the " St. Bartholomew of Privilege " : for the Constituent Assembly had already been alarmed by sporadic insurrections among the peasants, who were eagerly awaiting their release from economic slavery and saw little hope of its achievement by the middle class legislators at Versailles. On the evening of August 3rd the Constituent Assembly listened to a report on these disquieting disturbances ; possible repression of them was suggested. Next evening, the 4th, the project of a stern warning to the peasants was actually being discussed when, with theatrical suddenness, certain of the privileged began to renounce their privileges : and virtuous aristocrats, led by de Noailles, the tears of generous excitement raining down their cheeks, vied with each other in abandoning their rights, or at least those of their friends. Feudalism abolished ! All that France really needed, achieved within two months of the " opening " of the Revolution, and by the free gift of the threatened classes. It was an

[1] The use of titles was forbidden on June 19th, 1790.

inspiring thought ; and the incautious[1] might be deceived into supposing that the continued violence of the Revolution must have been the underground work of secret societies egging on " the people," who had already obtained all that they could rightly expect.

An inspiring thought ; but unfortunately it was false. The 4th of August abolished scarcely a third of the feudal system. Only those seignorial rights which implied personal servitude were regularly abolished (though not till Louis XVI had brought himself to sanction the decree on November 3rd). The " *droits réels* " were presumed legal and proof of usurpation made impracticable ; they were to be held due until they were redeemed, and owing to the high assessment redemption too was made extremely difficult, often impossible. The tithe, abolished in principle, was " provisionally maintained," and was actually collected until January 1st, 1791. Hence lively disappointment among the peasants to whom the Constituent Assembly had so trumpeted the " destruction of feudalism " on August 4th. And this lively disappointment and discontent goes a long way to explain those sporadic *Jacqueries* (peasant riots and *chateau*-burnings) which in varying degrees certain writers[2] are disposed to attribute to the hidden hand of secret agitators.

It was in deference to this widespread disillusionment among the peasants that on June 18th, 1792—that is, even before the *journée* of August 10th—the Legislative Assembly carried one stage further this progressive destruction of the feudal principle, by abolishing, without compensation, all contingent rights (*droits casuels*) unless they were demonstrably owed as payment for grants of land, in which case they could be redeemed.

[1] For example, Mrs. Webster.
[2] And to a very high degree Mrs. Webster.

Next, on the 25th August following, all feudal dues were abolished, without indemnity, unless their original titles could be produced ; and since these were usually at least as old as the XIVth or XVth centuries, to produce them was not often possible. Thus on the very threshold of the Republic the peasants were rallied to its cause.

Finally, on the 17th July, 1793, the Terror suppressed even those dues whose original titles were still in existence.

It took four years, then, to destroy feudalism, but at last feudalism was dead. And, as we said just now of the establishment of order, this achievement too of releasing France from the infinitely oppressive feudal burden would by itself give to the Revolution a meaning and a justification.

Concurrently, and, to a large extent, in consequence of the abolition of the feudal burden, there was in operation throughout these years an immense change in the ownership of land. The property of the clergy and of the *émigrés* had passed, and cheaply, into other hands. Many of the buyers had no doubt been nobles or members of the prosperous middle class, but more had been peasants. (An analysis by Lecarpentier of the sales in eighteen different districts shows 220,000 peasant buyers against 140,000 of the middle classes.) And the land which early in the Revolution was sold in large lots, was soon cut up into innumerable small holdings. The peasant was in possession of the land ! This was the land settlement of the Revolution.

Such a change had never been the avowed or even conscious purpose of the Revolution at its outset. But it had come ; and may be considered, as we have seen, as the corollary of that destruction of feudalism which had been one of the Revolution's two primary purposes. Both achievements, that of the conscious purpose and that of its equally important pendant or corollary, were confirmed and made permanent by Napoleon. Together they lie at the roots of the régime of to-day, and from 1799 onwards the peasant-in-possession has been, within certain limits, the most powerful conservative force in modern France. Any government that will guarantee his possession the peasant will support ; against any threat to it he will fight to the death. The Bourbon Restoration under Charles X was to show signs of challenging the Revolution's land settlement with the rest of its work, but his co-heirs of the Revolution, the middle classes, had overthrown the Bourbons for the last time before the peasant had realised the threat to his own share in the legacy of 1789. The new revolutionaries in 1848, and again in 1871, were to threaten the peasant's legacy and each time he successfully took arms to defend it. So profoundly, in this matter, had the Revolution transformed France.

Besides abolishing the feudal dues, the Revolution had attempted to introduce equality into taxation. The basis of its system was to have been a just contribution from all, where the *ancien régime* had exempted, as we saw, the only classes which were qualified to pay. Unfortunately—largely because both collectors and assessors of taxes were elected—the system had never functioned. At the beginning of 1793 there were 176 millions of francs still owing on the year 1791 and 296 millions on 1792. But here, too, Napoleon confirmed and rendered operative the effort of the Revolution. He appoints his own collectors and receivers, employing six thousand officials in place of the two hundred thousand of the *ancien régime*. The State must have its income, and there are no arrears. But the farmer pays at worst not more than 21 per cent. of his income. Under the *ancien régime* in dues and taxes he lost 81 per cent.

Feudalism had been abolished primarily in the interest of the peasant and small farmer. This, too, was the class which profited principally by the introduction of equality into taxation. For the middle classes equality had meant the levelling of the social barriers, and by this levelling the way was to be opened not only for the middle classes, but for the poorest ; for Masséna or Ney to the position of Marshal of France. Equality in this sense Napoleon confirmed by the " career open to talent " : " in my service all men are equal." And his Legion of Honour must not be mistaken for a violation of the principle of social equality. That principle requires merely that birth should not disqualify. To reward merit, provided that the reward itself does not (like a hereditary peerage) create exclusive privilege and therefore disqualification, is not to deny equality.

Social equality and order, these had been the aims of the Revolution and had been realised. Military glory, and the transference of the soil to the peasant, this further, the Revolution had achieved. And it may be noted here that the Revolution had founded the system of national education of modern France. The *ancien régime* had not been at any pains to educate those who paid its taxes, but the Convention, in the very crisis of the Revolution, had founded the Écoles Centrales, the École Normale, and the Institute of France, besides reorganising the Natural History Museum and the Collège de France. It is true that there are great goods beside these ; great goods which the Revolution signally failed to bring about. Political equality, for example, and liberty. But these were goods which, though it could make battle-cries of them, it did not strongly desire ; which Frenchmen have seldom desired strongly.

Thus the " passive citizens " of the middle class régime of 1789-1792 showed for a long while little desire for the vote ; and the campaign for equality of suffrage was carried on, with little support from the excluded, by middle class intellectuals, a general staff without an army. Even of the " active " citizens only an average of eleven per cent. made use of their right to vote.

Universal suffrage (excepting only domestic servants) followed the insurrection of August 10th, 1792 : it had indeed been made inevitable, even before the insurrection by the decree of August 1st, which gave " active " citizenship to the armies. At the elections for the Convention, ending in September, 1792, the vote was used by perhaps about twenty-five per cent. of the electorate.

But the Directorial Constitution of the year III reverted to limited suffrage : to be an elector " of the second degree " a citizen must be twenty-five years old and possess property worth two hundred days' work per annum, or be a tenant of a dwelling worth a hundred and fifty days' work or of a country property worth two hundred days' work per annum. And on the whole the nation concerned itself remarkably little with the change.

Napoleon, while rendering apparent homage to the principle of universal suffrage, in fact annihilated the electoral system altogether. For though the vote was universal as in 1792, the electors in each *arrondissement* obtained only with it the right to elect one-tenth of their own number, from among whom the public officers of the *arrondissement* would be appointed. The lists of the *arrondissements* reduced each to one-tenth made up the departmental list, and those of the departments,

similarly reduced, the national list of the eligible to such
" national public functions " as that of deputy. Clearly
to require an *arrondissement* to elect a tenth of its own
number meant that it could exercise no choice whatever :
no party could be altogether excluded : probably all who
could read and write respectably would have to be
selected. Napoleon had not so much suppressed political
equality as reduced all to a dead equality of political
impotence. But, rightly or wrongly, it was a price which,
in return for the conquests which Napoleon had ensured
the Revolution, the Revolution was very willing to pay.
And as for liberty, even had France desired it, it was
scarcely possible yet. Between 1792 and 1815 France
was all but ceaselessly involved in European war, and
liberty, as we know, does not prosper in a country
involved in European war. Social liberty did not exist
under the Napoleonic administration, and in the
tribunate and legislative body of the Empire political
liberty was equally unknown. Political liberty was
obliterated by Napoleon ; and yet in spite of that, or
perhaps we should say because of that, he remains the
heir and champion of the Revolution. And the solid
achievement of this first era of the Revolution remains
incontestable and astonishing.

What was the Revolution ? We are now beginning to
be in a position to answer that question. I have drawn
attention already to the confusion of thought which
attaches to those familiar words " the French Revolution." For, unfortunately, by " the French Revolution "
is usually understood, quite loosely, all the events
recorded by the history of France within the years 1789
to 1799. And so " the French Revolution " becomes not
only all the cruel and extravagant measures, but actually
all the counter-revolutionary measures of those years.

"The French Revolution" is la Vendée and the *émigrés* as well as the *noyades* and the Place de la Guillotine. "The French Revolution" is, in a word, both Marat and Charlotte Corday.

And this interpretation of the Revolution is more than, as it might appear at first sight, mere contradiction or irrelevance. For thanks to it it is fatally easy for its historians, selecting whether maliciously or at random from the vast complexity of its records, to represent the Revolution as sanguinary, meaningless, and incoherent. Concentration upon the inessential ; that is the upshot of this confusion. And perhaps the form which this almost universal concentration upon the inessential most commonly, and most excusably, takes, is the identification of the Revolution with the Terror ; or, a little more comprehensively and a good deal more plausibly, with the Idealogues and the Terror. This last is in fact, as we shall see, what de Maistre and the philosophers of the Restoration understood by the Revolution. But for the man in the street the Revolution is still no more than the Terror. Now in truth, as we have seen, the Terror was the point at which the Revolution, shaking itself free from the sterile effort of the Idealogues to break altogether with the past and to perpetuate privilege, began solidly to achieve its purpose. But how easy it is to see the Terror as no more than its own surface, "the red fool-fury of the Seine," the panic cruelty of a nation threatened without and within.

There is a classic but precisely analogous confusion with regard to Greek civilisation. The common identification of Hellenism with a certain abnormality in sexual morals, although consecrated by centuries of usage, is entirely unscientific : for, as Professor Gilbert Murray has pointed out, the remarkable thing about Hellenism is not that there was so much of this particular abnormality but that, on that oasis which Greek civilisation made among the surrounding wastes of barbarism, there was so little. And in the same way the astonishing thing about the French Revolution is that it was with such little bloodshed that it accomplished such prodigious and such rapid changes. So great a convulsion of society as this Revolution must produce formidable explosions and give rise to formidable passions far removed from their original cause ; and the more violent the original convulsion the greater will be the distance from it at which its consequences, direct and indirect, will appear, and the harder will it be to disengage the originating causes from their more or less accidental results, and so to seize the *reality* of the forces in operation. When volcanic forces are at work underground it is easy enough to detect some of the innumerable fissures which will open upon the earth's surface, but these may well be a long way distant from the seat of the disturbance. To a superhuman and spiritual vision the French Revolution may be everything which resulted from the explosion of 1789, one incalculable whole of suffering and activity in which there are no irrelevances since no part is less significant than another. But scientific study must inevitably select the central and structural. And that selection must be made upon some principle, if we are not to be driven back once more upon the unphilosophic partisanship of almost all the historians of the last century which selects for emphasis from " the Revolution," considered as the mere agglomeration of ten years' events, whatever phases, malevolent or idealist, best suit its own thesis. And I submit that the principle on which we disengage the essential Revolution can only be the selection of its efforts to achieve the aims with which it originated. In other words the Revolution is not the history of France in the ten years from 1789, not even, though this view has the authority of Aulard, merely the Declaration of Rights and the efforts to achieve it, *but the French people's deep and instinctive sense of the need of certain changes, and their efforts, beneath the distractions first of Ideology and then of foreign and domestic war, to accomplish them.*

We will thus summarise this Revolution at the stage which it has now reached. The Revolution had been an instinctive national movement, which existed long before 1789, to establish order, primarily in the interests of the middle classes, and equality, primarily in the interests of the peasant. This movement was cut across in the first three years after 1789 by two distracting forces: first, the attempt of the Idealogues to break loose altogether from the past and to found a state upon abstract principles untempered by experience ; second, the attempt of the middle classes, who alone were the conscious initiators of the Revolution in its early stages, to establish themselves in succession to the nobility as a new privileged class. Thus neither the Declaration of Rights nor the Constitution of 1791 was the essential Revolution ; the essential Revolution in these early stages was a slow instinctive movement outpaced and obscured by these artificialities, and has no landmarks in it between the taking of the Bastille or October 6th, 1789, and August 10th, 1792. Then, broadly speaking, August, 1792, or at least the beginning of the Terror, is the point at which the essential Revolution becomes conscious of itself ; and this general truth is expressed in three different aspects of the Terror ; the Terror, that is, marks, first, the first thorough consideration of the claims of the class which had not consciously contributed to the opening of the Revolution, that is, the first thorough consideration of the principle of equality ; secondly, the release of the Revolution from Ideology and therefore the commencement of most of its genuine achievement; which, thirdly, involved in many instances, as a *sine quâ non* of its being, a return to the traditions of the *ancien régime*. In 1799 the despot closed this first stage of the Revolution, and he closed it by confirming and completing all the efforts on which the nation had genuinely set store. Equality and order, together with glory and the transference of the land to the small owner, two conquests which had not been among the avowed motives of the Revolution, he guaranteed—at the price of liberty, a price which the nation was only too willing to pay.

CHAPTER V

THE ATTACK ON THE REVOLUTION
(1814-1830)

TAKEN by itself, what I have just written of the relation
of Napoleon to the Revolution would give Napoleon too
great an importance. For Napoleon was emphatically
not an independent force meeting, and moulding, the
Revolution from without. Napoleon was made by the
Revolution. Obscure forces in it raised him up to satisfy
its own needs : and had there been no Napoleon to
determine and consolidate the Revolution, the Revolution must have found some other to play his rôle.[1]
Throughout his career it was upon the revolutionary idea,
crystallised for this while and become static, that his
power was based. The Revolution did not surrender to
the Empire, for the Empire was the Revolution. And
when the imperial superstructure collapsed in 1814 the
revolutionary idea became apparent once more beneath
it, essentially unmodified by its period of immobility
but facing an unknown future.

The Revolution is continuous. Nothing came to an
end in 1799. All that is to be said is that in 1799 the
Revolution began to consolidate and to immobilise, and
that in 1814 one thing had become clear—that it could
no longer remain immobile.

[1] Sieyès and Talleyrand had even thought of Ferdinand of Brunswick.

The ghost of the Bourbon monarchy sitting crowned upon the grave thereof ! What is the history of that resurrection ? As usually presented, these years from 1814 to 1830 are quite exceptionally intricate and obscure. In reality they possess a unity quite exceptionally seizable and illuminating. Between 1814 and 1830 the revolutionary settlement was violently attacked by a party which aimed at nothing less than a return to feudalism, to the *ancien régime*. *The Revolution of* 1789 *had passed to the defensive*. That, in a sentence, is the history of 1814 to 1830. Beneath the apparent complexity of the political struggle there are two parties and two only ; one the party of the *ancien régime*, the feudalists, as we may call them ; the other, the party of the revolutionary settlement—we shall see a little later why, to be accurate, we must speak, not of the party of the Revolution but of the party of the revolutionary settlement—and this is a party of the middle classes. For of the two beneficiaries under the revolutionary settlement these only emerged to fight for it ; their co-heirs, the peasant classes, remained unconscious and indifferent ; the struggle, though it so closely concerned them, went on over their heads. The defence of the Revolution was in the hands of the middle classes. It was only, as we saw, abnormal circumstances which in 1789 had made of them a revolutionary force, and in returning thus to their natural function, which is conservative, they became a more formidable and permanent power in politics. By the Revolution of 1830 the assault upon the Revolution of 1789 was finally defeated. Henceforth the revolutionary settlement is to be part of the permanent structure of France, and the revolutionary idea, in the form in which we have so far known it, becomes definitely a *conservative* force : from 1830

onwards until to-day it stands upon the defensive no
longer against the past but against the future, against
a new and more formidable assault ; the assault of the
New Revolution.

The struggle of the feudal party against the revolutionary settlement ! It is indispensable to retain this
clue to the intricate political manœuvres of the Restoration. Without it they are more than obscure ; they are
unintelligible. The feudalist party, for example, is
traditionally labelled " Ultra-Royalist," and the middle
class party of the Revolution " Liberal "; and yet when
in September, 1816, Louis XVIII dissolved the Ultra-
Royalist chamber by royal ordinance we find the " Ultra-
Royalists " protesting bitterly against this exercise of
royal prerogative, while the " Liberals " (who, further,
are essentially conservative—of the revolutionary *status
quo*) defend it as hotly against the presumed privileges
of parliamentary government. The truth is, of course,
that both Crown and Parliament, and their respective
rights, are no more than the instruments of the conflicting parties quite incidental to the essential struggle ;
so that the feudalist party, when the Crown is allied with
its enemy, will cheerfully speak the language of democracy, while the party of the revolutionary settlement,
as long as the Crown is behind it, will be found cham-
pioning prerogative as hotly as Strafford.

A short analysis of the political history of the Restoration in the light of this central struggle will best illustrate
and explain a period without understanding which can
be understood neither the conflict which has preceded
it nor that which is to follow. But first let me say something of the intellectual assault by which the political
assault upon the Revolution of 1789 was accompanied.

In the literature of the Restoration there are three

prominent writers all of whom represent not only a
militant denial of what they take to be the principles of
the Revolution but a fierce and positive return to what
they take to be the principles of the *ancien régime*. These
are de Maistre, Bonald, and Lammenais, and, in spite
of variations in detail, the thesis of their work is essentially so much the same that it is reasonable to summarise
it as one whole. It is a destructive, and, as far as it goes,
a convincing, criticism of eighteenth century thought
and of the Revolution which it assumes to be its expression ; an attack, that is, first on the philosophers,
and primarily on Rousseau and Voltaire, and secondly
on the " *apriorisme* " of the Idealogues.

The new mediævalists did not find very much difficulty
in demolishing the principal doctrines of Rousseau. Thus
Rousseau had taught that man is naturally good and is
corrupted by society. De Maistre and Bonald replied
that, on the contrary, man is naturally bad ; original sin
is the ultimate truth ; and man is saved by society.
"We are bad by nature, we are made good by society.
. . . . Those who . . . have begun by supposing that
we are born good . . . are like architects who, about to
build an edifice, should suppose that the stones appear
from the quarry ready cut and the wood ready hewn
from the forest," says Bonald. So far from the artificial
restraints imposed by society being instruments of corruption, do but remove them and society itself gives
place to chaos. The Revolution itself attests this truth.

The disciples of Rousseau had maintained that society
is founded upon a contract ; men having come together
and agreed to submit their individual wills to a general
will. But, objects Bonald, a contract presupposes a society.
He imagines primitive isolated families meeting instinctively to face a common danger ; the ablest individual

inevitably takes command (*monarch*) ; the next ablest
associate themselves with him (*ministers*) ; the rest obey
(*subjects*). And here at once is—society. Such a society
is not artificial and voluntary, but natural and inevitable.
So far from there being a contract between monarch and
subjects the subjects are " only too happy to have found
a saviour," they have accepted gratefully whatever
conditions, in their interest, he chooses to impose. The
time for written constitutions is later. A constitution
must exist before it is written. " *La nature constitue,
l'homme ne sait qu'organiser* " (Bonald). That it was
purely *a priori* was precisely the reason for the failure
of the constitution of 1791.

Again the disciples of Rousseau had held that authority
is derived from the people and its general will, and that
as there is a " natural man," so there is a " natural
morality." It was not difficult to reply that there is no
such thing as a " general will " of the people, only an
aggregate of conflicting individual wills.[1] And further
that, if there be a natural " morality," what is its
standard ? Is it to be Rousseau's morality or Voltaire's
or Robespierre's ? For all the philosophers are rival
prophets. And the philosophers' Revolution, which
began with universal toleration, went on to the cult of
Reason.

And the Revolution itself is for these writers no more
than Rousseau put into practice, the *apriorisme of*
Ideology deducing its constitution, like a school-problem
in mathematics, from the general principles of a man who
had " shut his eyes to reality." The principles of the
Revolution then which were truths of "reason " are no
principles ; what is to take their place ? For, " whether
he wish it or not " (says Lammenais), " man must

[1] See, *e.g.*, Bonald : *Théorie du pouvoir*, Pt. I, Bk. I, cap. 10.

believe." In place of the truths of reason, which set up
no absolute and ultimate standard, only the ceaseless
conflict of individual opinion, these writers invoke the
permanent truth of authority, the authority of God.
With their proofs of the existence of God and of " the
truths of faith " we need not concern ourselves ; the
remarkable point is that these truths are shown to involve
not only orthodox religion but the whole of the *ancien
régime*, " God, Christ, mankind " ; " pope, priests,
laymen " ; " king, nobles, people." These are the
trinities upon which universe, church and state are based.
The only form in which church or state can harmonise
with the universe is in the mediæval form.

Now, broadly speaking, this destructive criticism of
eighteenth century rationalism and of the use to which it
was put by the Idealogues is unanswerable. And Bonald,
de Maistre, and Lammenais, saying in effect " this movement began with Ideology and resulted in the Terror
and therefore it is damned," give an illusory effect of
comprehensively discrediting the Revolution. The fallacy
of their attack is, of course, the assumption that the
Revolution is no more than eighteenth century rationalism
put into practice by Idealogues. Whereas, in fact, as we
have seen, the theory which preceded the Revolution,
and the theorists into whose clutches it fell at first, were
altogether distinct from the essential Revolution itself,
which they did but first " explain," and then pervert for
a while. The attack of Bonald and the rest upon the true
Revolution is not so much direct as indirect, and is best
illustrated not by its destructive criticism but by its
constructive theory of the permanent rightness of
mediæval society. Into this we cannot follow them here.
It is enough for our purposes to realise that what made
the attack of Bonald, de Maistre, and Lammenais,

coming just when it did, so formidable was that, essentially, what they invoke against the new order is—the *ancien régime*.

It is tempting here to go a little further into the literary history of the Restoration, so closely allied with its politics, and to show how this reaction against eighteenth century classicism in the interests of the old order passed over—in the hands of historians like Lamartine, Thierry, and Guizot, poets like Hugo, and painters like Delacroix—to the service of Romance and the new order. But I must go back to sketch in outline the political history of the Restoration in which took shape the mortal struggle between the Revolution and the *ancien régime*.

Louis XVIII returned to France pledged to the Charter of June, 1814. This charter retained intact the revolutionary-Napoleonic settlement—that is to say, the *social* and *administrative* organisation which guaranteed equality and order. There remained the problem of *political* organisation. Napoleon had solved, or shelved, that problem off hand by suppressing political liberty altogether. But now the difficulty reopens, and France has to manufacture for herself a constitution. This is to be an age of constitution-mongers. But we must be careful here. This void left by the revolutionary-Napoleonic settlement, the unsolved constitutional problem, is not the *cause* of the conflict which fills the years of the Restoration, although at first sight it may appear to be so. It is its *symptom*. The two rival parties are not at issue about so trifling a matter as this unfilled political void : they are at issue as to whether the solid, social and administrative settlement of the Revolution, inevitably left *in situ* by the Charter, shall, or shall not, be replaced by a resurrection of the *ancien régime*. The return of privilege ! That is the avowed purpose of the feudal party. *Equality* is the conquest of the Revolution which they have marked down for destruction. *Order* is not, cannot be, openly attacked. But order must have perished with equality: for the return to privilege implied the return to decentralisation, to the great landowner instead of the *préfet*. And as they manœuvre for position in this central conflict in which the foundations of France, her social and therefore her administrative order, are at stake, the matter for the moment in dispute is usually some attempt of one or other to determine what shall fill the void left by the Charter when it abandoned the political organisation of Napoleon. For the forms with which that void may be filled will go a long way either to facilitate or to preclude the wholesale restoration of the *ancien régime*.

In the matter of political organisation the Charter left a void. Now I do not mean that the Charter did not prescribe anything in the nature of a political organisation. It certainly prescribed definitely enough the framework of a political organisation, but within that framework it left certain essential problems unsolved. And the constitution of the Charter must be meaningless until these questions were answered ; for upon their answer depended its whole character and effect. This constitution was modelled with servile exactness upon the English. Government consisted of king, chamber of peers, and chamber of deputies. Control of the budget by the lower chamber, responsibility of ministers, freedom of the press—the system was carried across the Channel, lock, stock and barrel. But two principal questions remained unsolved. Even in England they were unanswered ; or rather the answer to one, modified during the long reign of George III, was in a state of flux ; the answer to the other was about to be in debate.

First, the relation of the king to the elective chamber. Must the king choose his ministers from the party which was in a majority ? *Second*, how precisely was the chamber of deputies to be elected ? The Charter prescribed the minimum qualification for the suffrage—the payment of 300 francs in direct taxation. But it went no further, said nothing of the mode of election. And even the 300 francs' qualification was very soon to be challenged. Here then, in these two omissions, lay ready prepared the field for a combat to the death between the principle of the old order and the principle of the new.

The Restoration may conveniently be divided into three periods. Of these the first covers the life of the so-called *chambre introuvable* (August, 1815, to September, 1816), during which a feudalist majority is neutralised by the alliance of the crown with the party of the revolutionary settlement.

This first chamber of the Restoration was elected (August, 1815) according to the electoral system of the Empire under the influence of the Hundred Days and Napoleon's second defeat and abdication, and it contained a large feudalist majority. Louis XVIII mistook it for a royalist chamber and dubbed it the *chambre introuvable*. He was soon undeceived. It was not long before he realised that this chamber was not *plus royaliste*, but *plus feudaliste, que le roi*. King and chamber remained in accord while it established or encouraged a preliminary white terror of vengeance against both regicides of the Convention and leading functionaries of the Empire, whose principal official feature was the *cours prévôtales* of five judges with a military president for the summary trial of sedition. But the feudal majority in this first flush of power regained went on further—to attack already the revolutionary settlement. It not only proposed to abolish several institutions guaranteed by the Charter, including the University ; but actually demanded the restitution of the *biens nationaux*. The Revolutionary Land Settlement challenged so soon ! This was the cloven hoof with a vengeance. "Arresting the Revolution," Chateaubriand complacently called it. " By banishing the regicides and arresting the sale of the national domains the chamber has arrested the Revolution." But the Chamber of Peers, which consisted largely of ex-functionaries of the Empire, put an end to the attempt for the moment. The feudalist party, its ardour nothing abated, was soon at loggerheads with the king.

Louis XVIII was alarmed. He had realised already that the feudalist party (which for a moment he had mistaken for royalist) was determined to destroy the revolutionary settlement. But the revolutionary settlement, as we saw, had been preserved by the Charter as the basis of the Restoration ; and it did not require an extravagantly clear insight nor an extravagantly cautious temperament to suspect that the removal of its present basis, even were a substitute to be furnished from the *ancien régime*, might prove to be an architectural operation which the Bourbon Restoration, already a somewhat unsteady edifice, would be unable to survive. The king had accordingly selected all but three of his ministers from the minority in the chamber which, for various reasons self-interested and doctrinaire, was prepared to uphold the guarantee given by the Charter to the settlement of the Revolution. This party—and this becomes important later—was inevitably a party of compromise : for the revolutionary settlement embodied in a Bourbon monarchy could be nothing but a compromise. It is the party of the Charter's revolutionary settlement. This was a glaring compromise, and those who were familiar with the idiosyncrasies of the French intellect must have foreseen that its authority would not be lasting. And no sooner had the king turned to this party for his ministers than the feudalist majority (ultra-royalist, as it is usually labelled) protested in impassioned chorus against this arbitrary exercise of royal authority, while on behalf of the minority, in power thanks to the king, Royer-Collard formulated a doctrinaire theory of " independent royalty." The unreality of this constitutional controversy was apparent even to those who took part in it. " Soon," wrote Chateaubriand, himself a gorgeous partisan of the *ancien régime*, in *de la Monarchie selon la Charte*, " these ' liberals ' who are now doing their best to introduce arbitrary government, may be taxing the crown with crime for the self-same arbitrary measures which they now advise it." He might have made the same criticism, with the necessary inversions, of his own party. For the attitude of each to the crown and its prerogative depended entirely upon the side taken by the crown in their life and death struggle. And the majority of the feudal party, miscalled royalist, was probably just as ready to sacrifice Louis XVIII if he stood between them and the Restoration of privilege, as were many of the *émigrés* of 1791 to sacrifice Louis XVI when it came to a choice between his safety and their intrigue.

The second of the two omissions in the Charter to which I referred above was not slower in influencing the struggle. Early in 1816 the feudalist majority passed its electoral law through the Chamber of Deputies— only to see it defeated in the Chamber of Peers. This exceedingly instructive measure proposed to introduce election in two degrees, in the *canton* and in the *département*, and for the *canton* to reduce the qualification from 300 francs to 50 francs. This would have meant an increase of nearly two millions in the total number of electors. The king and the middle class minority adhered stubbornly to direct election and the 300 francs qualification (which meant less than 100,000 voters). The feudal party demands an enormous increase in the electorate, the party of the revolutionary settlement is for extremely limited rights ! This is at first sight a strange enough reversal of rôles, even if we have not gone out of our way to make it stranger by labelling the rivals royalist and liberal. The truth is that it is but a repetition of the phenomenon which we noticed at the time of the election to the States-General in 1789. What was practically manhood suffrage was accorded then because, the threat to the *ancien régime* coming from the middle classes, it was hoped that their vote would be diluted by the immense peasant suffrage, which might be expected to be still subject to the influence of the great landowners. Precisely the same manœuvre is repeated in 1816 and with precisely the same motives. A limited property vote is a middle class vote, a wider suffrage will obliterate the middle class influence ; and it must be remembered that in 1816 as in 1789 the anti-feudal cause was in the hands of the middle classes alone. And the hope that reviving feudalism might once more influence a small farmers' vote was no doubt also operative ; for the electoral project of the feudalists in 1816 must be considered in conjunction with their demand for decentralisation. and for the transference of local authority from the prefect to the great proprietor. The situation had now reached a deadlock. And on September 5th, 1816, was published the king's dissolution of the Chamber ;

it met, as we have already seen, with precisely the same indignantly " democratic " criticism from the feudal party as had been already evoked by his selection of ministers.

The second of the three periods of which I have spoken extends over the four years from September 1816 to February 1820, during which the party of the revolutionary settlement was genuinely in power.

The new chamber met in November, 1816. It contained a huge majority for the party of the revolutionary settlement ; which majority Decazes and Royer-Collard proceeded at once to employ for the perpetuation of middle class political influence. On February 5th, 1817, their Franchise Bill passed the two Chambers. It is remarkable that during this period the advent of one or other party to power is invariably closely followed by a new Franchise Law, designed to remodel the electoral process in its own interest. The middle class law of 1817 required a voter to be thirty years of age and to pay 300 francs in direct taxation ; and provided that the electors should assemble in the capital of the department (where the wealthy middle classes could best influence the elections). The Chamber was to be renewed by one-fifth every year. The middle class party could now count itself seated beside Louis XVIII upon the throne. And almost at once it began to suffer the fate which so often attends parties which become too powerful. It began to split.

During 1817 the ministry was occupied in restoring the finances of the State by a system of regular and audited budgets, and in attempting to pay off the war claims of the allies and accelerate their evacuation of French territory. The fissures began to open next year. The political history of these next two years deserves careful attention, for it is intricate and its intricacy is capable of obscuring the essential unity of the conflict in progress throughout the Restoration.

The middle class party which, in alliance with the crown, through the Charter, had been concerned to guarantee the revolutionary settlement was, as we have already seen, essentially a compromise. On the right of this central party were those opponents who, like Chateaubriand, desired a whole-hearted return to the *ancien régime*; on the left those who demanded not merely the maintenance of the revolutionary settlement but a return to the forms, and perhaps even the methods, of the Revolution; the revolutionary settlement, in fact, without the Bourbon Charter; republicans, these, of various shades, like Manuel and Cavaignac and Lafayette. And since the French intellect neither likes nor understands a compromise, power was certain to pass sooner or later to one or other of these two extremes. It began at once to show signs of moving towards the left, the extreme party—of the Revolution, not merely the Revolution's settlement—" Jacobins " as the feudalists called them. In 1817 and again in 1818, at the partial renewal of the Chamber, this party gained seats—in opposition to the ministerialists. The feudalists, although they had of course no intention of permitting their extremer adversaries, the " Jacobins," to obtain power, welcomed the embarrassment of the government—" better a Jacobin than a ministerialist," said the *Drapeau Blanc*—and they did their best to embitter the relations between these two wings of the middle class champions of the revolutionary settlement. Smiling, no doubt, to himself, Chateaubriand wrote of Decazes in the *Conservateur* as the persecutor of the revolutionaries.

And gradually the government began to dissolve into its component parts. After all, this party of the Charter and the revolutionary settlement contained both those who, like the Duc de Richelieu, accepted the revolutionary settlement because it was embodied in the Charter, and those who, like Royer-Collard and Guizot, accepted the Charter because it embodied the revolutionary settlement. And in face of this onslaught of the uncompromising left—" the re-awakening of the Terror" as it soon appeared to the Tsar Alexander I—these two elements inevitably tended to adopt divergent attitudes. Those who, like Richelieu, belonged to what the jargon of politics would call " the right centre," showed signs of coalescing with the feudalists ; they were for retaliation against " the Jacobins " and a modification of the electoral law of 1817 in the feudal interest. On the other hand, what would be called " the left centre " was for maintaining its central position, that is, the permanence of the revolutionary settlement within the Bourbon monarchy ; and Louis XVIII sided with it. On December 28th, 1818, he allowed Richelieu to retire.

The ministry, reconstituted under Dessolles and Decazes, began at once to experience the discomforts of compromise in French politics. The party of Richelieu had frankly gone over to the feudalists ; the "Jacobins" continued to reject the government's compromise, and in effect to demand not merely the revolutionary settlement but the Revolution. Decazes made a show of resistance. He even created seventy-three new peers, to give himself a fictitious majority in the upper chamber. But within a year he had yielded. It was to the feudal party that he determined to capitulate. And in November, 1819, his more stubborn colleagues were cast overboard and Decazes appeared at the head of a new cabinet, pledged to remodel in the interests of the feudalists his own party's electoral law of 1817 to ensure whose safety he had less than a year ago forced Richelieu to retire. He had betrayed the party of the revolutionary settlement without placating the feudalists. His fall was a question of weeks. And the murder of the king's nephew, the Duc de Berri, three months later, on February 13th, 1820, was no more than the occasion, not the cause, of his fall. He did not "slip in the blood he had shed," as one of his opponents engagingly suggested : he fell because, from the moment when he abandoned the electoral law of 1817, he had ceased to represent either of the rival principles.

The champions of the revolutionary settlement had failed to retain power precisely because, standing for that settlement only, and not for the Revolution itself, they represented a compromise ; and in French politics compromise is disaster. But the fact that during their four years in authority it became evident that the middle class heirs of the Revolution had fallen apart into two rival wings must not be allowed to blind us to the undeniable unity of the struggle as a whole. During these four years, as before and after them, the matter at issue remains unchanged : shall the *ancien régime* be restored ; is a dead thing to come back to life ? And after 1820, as before 1816, we need not concern ourselves with this schism among the partisans of the new order. For from 1820 to 1830 the men of the *ancien régime* are in power, and making full use of their opportunity, and in face of that danger the opposition, for practical purposes, closes its ranks.

The third of the three periods to which I have referred extends from February, 1820, until the Revolution of July, 1830, and represents the feudalists in power. For

clearness' sake I call it one period, because during these
ten years the feudalist party is all but uninterruptedly in
a position to carry out its supreme attempt to reconstruct
the *ancien régime*. To be more meticulous, but not nearer
the truth, we might subdivide this period either at 1824
—when, with the accession of Charles X, the crown, from
a passive instrument, becomes an energetic ally of the
feudalist cause—or at January, 1828, when for sixteen
months Charles X resigned himself with an ill grace to
substitute for the reaction a policy of reluctant concession under Martignac. But the ten years may be
much more reasonably and fruitfully considered as a
whole.

It is unnecessary to sketch the parliamentary history
of the decade. I will only summarise the principal and
typical measures by which the feudalists (whose real
leader logically enough was not Richelieu, late of the
compromise, but Villèle) did their best to re-establish the
two principal features of the feudal régime, a privileged
aristocracy of landowners and a privileged and influential
church. The destruction of equality ! Such is the theme
of these years. The destruction of order, as we saw, must
have followed it as a necessary consequence. Further,
we must note, in another aspect this struggle between
the feudal party and the middle classes was a struggle
between the new industrialism and the old agricultural
economy. If for this reason alone there could be no doubt
which party would finally triumph.

The dictatorship opened with the customary *revanche*,
the feudalist electoral law (April, 1820). By this the
number of deputies in the Chamber was increased from
258 to 430. The 258 who made up the original total, and
the fifth of the entire Chamber required by the annual
renewals, were to be elected, not in the capital of the

department, as the law of 1817 had prescribed in the interests of the middle classes, but in the *collèges d'arrondissement*, where the large landowners could best make their influence felt. The 172 new deputies required this year were to be elected in the departments by the most highly taxed (a quarter) of the whole body of electors. This change in effect gave a second vote to the country squire. And, voting under this system, the electorate obligingly returned a vast majority of feudalists.

It should be remembered that in 1823 the feudalists were able to force the king to intervene in Spain in the interests of absolutism. This was France's first considerable taste of glory since Waterloo, and was to be for a long while her last. It is of some importance, and we shall have to refer to it again a little later. Its significance for our immediate purpose may be best expressed in the words of Chateaubriand, to whose head glory mounted very readily. (He considered that the Spanish parade " restored France to military equality with the great powers of Europe.") " The victories of the Revolution are not effaced," he wrote, " but they no longer exercise a dangerous influence over the imagination. Other victories have ranged themselves between the throne of the Bourbons and that of the Usurper."

In 1825, being unable to restore the *biens nationaux* which were guaranteed by the Charter, the feudalists did what seemed to them the next best thing. They compensated the dispossessed *émigrés* with a milliard of francs. It was hoped that the money might be employed for the repurchase of landed estates. This not inconsiderable sum had been obtained by converting the interest on the national debt from five per cent. to three per cent. And as so many of the *rente*-holders belonged to the middle classes an incidental but satisfactory aspect of the measure was the discomfort it occasioned to the avowed enemies of the feudalist cause.

This attempt to assist the reconstitution of large estates should be considered in conjunction with a bill to amend the legislation of the Civil Code which had given to all children an equal share in an inherited estate. The new bill doubled the legal legacy to the eldest son in families which paid 3,000 francs in land tax. This measure, to the chagrin of the feudalists, was rejected in the Chamber of Peers. Had it passed it would naturally have assisted the growth of large landed estates and therewith the aristocracy of the *ancien régime*. Villèle, speaking in its defence, asserted that its sole motive was the encouragement of agriculture.

Education was passing into the control of the Church. A priest was Grand Master of the University. Guizot and Cousin were deprived of their chairs at the Sorbonne ; one because he was a Protestant, the other because he was a philosopher. For the Grand Master of the University disapproved of philosophy. Candidates for local office, civil or educational, were required to obtain an authorisation from their bishop. The law of sacrilege (1826) punished church robbery and other forms of sacrilege with death. This was a symbolic measure, announcing the intention to punish religious offences with special penalties.

At the election of November, 1827, a coalition of all the enemies of the *ancien régime*, whatever their mutual differences, decisively defeated the feudal party. Charles X sullenly accepted a ministry of compromise, or at least concession, under Martignac. Inevitably it satisfied no one, and least of all the king. In April, 1829, he dismissed it and with the utmost content proceeded, by an exercise of royal prerogative like that of Louis XVIII in 1816, to govern with a ministry openly hostile to the majority in the Chamber. But between the two instances there was one essential difference. On this occasion the Chamber had the nation behind it.

The occasion of the Revolution of July, 1830, was " the four ordinances " of Polignac ; its promoters were a comparatively small number, many of them republican, but agreeing wholeheartedly only in hatred of the Bourbons. But the *cause* of the Revolution, that which made it not only possible but inevitable, was the determination of the middle classes that the ghost of the *ancien régime* should once and for all be laid.

The Revolution was thus carried through by a handful of more or less convinced republicans in Paris, but control of it was speedily assumed by the group of deputies who represented, like the government of 1816 to 1820, the compromise of Royalists with the revolutionary settlement. This group of deputies it was which determined the offer of the crown to Louis Philippe—in return for a fresh guarantee of the revolutionary settlement through a mildly revised charter. And thus once more, though less obviously than in the compromise with the Bourbons, they triumphed alike over the feudalist reaction and the uncompromising Revolution which together had been too much for them in 1819 and 1820. The actual rising had been carried out largely by the new artisan class which was growing up in Paris with the Industrial Revolution ; but it had been diverted to the profit of the equally new class of industrial magnates. As a class the artisans were not yet powerful or self-conscious enough to control as well as occasion a Revolution. It will not be long before we hear of them again.

The Revolution of 1789 had finally triumphed. On the 26th July the *ancien régime* seemed upon the brink of complete restoration. On July 30th it was as dead as the Empire of the Grand Mogul. What new power had been set up in return for a genuine and convincing guarantee of the revolutionary settlement we shall see in a moment. The essential fact is that on July 30th, 1830, the revolutionary settlement becomes henceforth unquestionably the basis of modern France. Here, if anywhere, the history of the Revolution ends ; and here the history of France in the nineteenth century begins. At this point the revolutionary idea becomes permanently *conservative*. Only a negligible element in it, the republican tradition, survives as an aggressive and revolutionary force. I say a negligible element, for the solid achievement of the Revolution once assured, the Republic means no more than a change of forms. It is true that the July monarchy by which the revolutionary settlement is guaranteed is still something of a compromise, and the logical French instinct will inevitably be moved to complete the incorporation of the Revolution in the structure of society by proceeding to the Republic. But we shall not consider mere republicanism, this merely logical residue of a great movement, as deserving to rank as the revolutionary idea which we have thus far watched in mortal struggle first to achieve, and then to render lasting, its profound modification of French society. All that is essential then in the revolutionary idea becomes now a conservative force. Henceforth it is to be itself upon the defensive—against a new Revolution.

CHAPTER VI

ANTECEDENTS OF THE NEW REVOLUTION
(1830-1848)

LOUIS PHILIPPE was proclaimed king of the French on
August 7th, 1830, and the next important event in his
reign was the Revolution which dethroned him in 1848.
It is not too much to say that from the moment of his
accession that event was a constant factor in the policy
of all parties in France. And, this being so, it is remarkable that none of them foresaw its true nature. The
forces which were to make the year 1848 a decisive
turning-point in the history of France and of the world
were almost entirely overlooked until their emergence
during the Revolution itself. What all parties suspected
or foresaw was a Revolution of the kind which had just
taken place, a Revolution which might perhaps substitute the Republic for the house of Orleans ; not a
Revolution which would introduce a new principle to
the world. In fact there did take place in 1848 a Revolution of the former kind ; but immediately upon its
initiation there emerged the new force, to dispute the
control of it with the familiar principle, and so to determine both the distinctive character and the immense
significance of the Revolution.

But this the parties who occupy the political platform
of the time did not suspect. Their policy relates itself

only to the possibility of the logical republican continuation of the old Revolution ; it was altogether remote from the intellectual and material forces which were working secretly to prepare the new. But, given this very limited horizon, the rival policies are clear cut and intelligible ; and it will be sufficient for our purposes to disengage their essential meaning before we go on to consider the all but subterranean forces which were creating and moulding the new form of the revolutionary idea. And we need concern ourselves no more than this with the political records of the reign. For although, hitherto, a study of the revolutionary idea has proved to be all but a historical outline both of the first revolutionary period and of the Bourbon Restoration, henceforth the new element, and all that is vital in the revolutionary idea, moves underground, remote from the history of history books, and occupies the orthodox recorded page only with its emergence in the Revolutions themselves in 1848 and 1871 ; so that consequently it is only in 1848 and 1871 that a study of the revolutionary idea resembles once more an outline of history.

What then—we need trouble ourselves with them no more than this—were the respective attitudes of the official parties to this logical progress of the old Revolution towards the Republic, for this progress was the issue which principally occupied the official politics of the reign ? And it should be noted here that throughout the reign official politics, confined by the limited suffrage to a class whose interests and opinions were so largely the same, tended increasingly to become an affair of merely personal animosities and advancement, so that the two main programmes of which I speak tended more and more to be overlaid and obscured by what essentially were meaningless combinations. The personal predominance of Louis Philippe contributed to the same result. " Parties," observed de Tocqueville, " could not afford to be drawn into a policy very remote from the king's views if they wished to retain power ; and this toned down the party colours to trifling differences of shade, and their struggle to mere verbal controversies." What then, first, were the two broad rival policies which can be disengaged from the artificialities of the official politics of the reign ?

We have remarked already that any guarantee of the Revolution of 1789 by a monarchy must be essentially a compromise and that since the French intellect abhors the illogical there was bound to be a demand for the Republic as the logical completion of the Revolution. Further, such a demand must imply that the July monarchy was but a transitional stage, one step further than the Bourbon restoration along the road to the ultimate logical conclusion, but still no more than a step. And this was in effect the view of one party. This party held that Louis Philippe had been elected by the people, and might be dismissed by them whenever it should suit their convenience. This view could clearly be very easily developed, as the number of republicans increased, into the explicit proposition which I suggested above—that the monarchy was a transitional stage to the Republic. And as such it is admirably summarized in a passage from Victor Hugo's " Les Misérables ": " 1830 is a Revolution stopped half way . . . now logic ignores the ' almost ' as the sun ignores a candle." It is this pitiless logic, applied to affairs as well as to intellectual processes, which has given France so many brilliant historians and such a disastrous history.

The other party represented the governmental policy of the reign. In its view the July monarchy was founded upon a contract between king and people, each of whom was henceforth dependent upon the other. The contract had put an end to the divine right of kings, but it precluded equally the sovereignty of the people. In other words, the July monarchy was not a transitional, but a final, stage. And this party, dimly suspecting 1848, adopted what earned the *soubriquet* of "the policy of resistance," inaugurated by Casimir-Périer and continued by Guizot. This policy defined itself during the constant disturbances of the early years of the reign, and although theoretically it did not disapprove of reform, it came to regard any concession to liberty as a step towards the dark possibilities ahead of it. "The principle of the Revolution of July," said Casimir-Périer, on March 17, 1831, "is the resistance of the sovereign power to any aggression." "Against the spirit of Revolution," said Guizot, some years later, "the government is bound to wage a perpetual war."

Such then were the rival policies which occupied the Chamber during the July monarchy. But they contributed remarkably little, either positively or negatively, to the Revolution of 1848. As we shall see when we examine it more closely, what we call the Revolution of 1848 embodies at least three distinct movements.

First : A ubiquitous, instinctive *impatience* with the ingloriousness of the July monarchy ; the boredom of a nation ; a weary distaste for the materialism and corruption of the Orleans régime, and more particularly for the conspicuous ingloriousness of its foreign policy. This is what made a successful Revolution possible, but this alone could not have carried a Revolution through. It was responsible for the first two days' disturbance— *à bas Guizot.* On the third was heard the cry *Vive la République.* How was it that by 1848 the nation as a whole was profoundly weary of the middle class monarchy, so that Lamartine could speak of " the Revolution of contempt " ?

By far the most important element in this contempt was the profound dissatisfaction of France with the inglorious foreign policy of its rulers. There was other reason for contempt, it is true. For the whole system of government had become commercialised ; and the *enrichissez-vous* of Guizot seemed not only the golden rule of commerce but of politics and literature as well. De Tocqueville puts the situation vividly. " Posterity," he observes in his remarkable *Souvenirs,* " will perhaps never realise to what an extent the government of that time had come to resemble a limited company in industry which undertakes all its operations with a view to the profit to be extracted from them by the shareholders." This mercantile spirit had invaded and corrupted literature as well. It was no longer the vulgar rich who aped or fawned upon the literary lion : under the July monarchy values had shifted and after the vast profits of a successful *roman* it was the proud boast of the literary lion that now he almost ranked with the vulgar rich. The era of the *roman-feuilleton,* this, when Dumas hawked for vast prices the tales he proudly classed as " merchandise " ; when Balzac demanded the state purchase of the works of those authors who " presented commerce with possibilities of exploitation " (his own he valued at the remarkable figure of two million francs), and when Eugène Suë at once corrupted and exploited his newspaper public with the lubricities of the *Mystères de Paris* and the *Sept Péchés Capitaux.*

Corruption was ubiquitous. " The nation," remarks de Tocqueville, " had conceived for the government a tranquil contempt, which was mistaken for trustful and unquestioning submission." But the discontent which touched all the nation, and touched it closely, was a matter of foreign policy.

For centuries the tradition of France had been a glorious foreign policy. Glory, rather than her material interests, was her passion. "Your policy is founded on reasoning, ours on sentiment," the Prince Napoleon remarked proudly to an Englishman in 1863. As we have seen, the Idealogue attempt to cut loose from the tradition failed very quickly ; and it was the promise of *la gloire* which established the power alike of Robespierre, Barras, and Napoleon. Then Waterloo ; and France a humiliated outcast from Europe. But the traditional passion endured. The dictatorship of Europe ! The ambition is shared by Frenchmen of every party. "*Il faut que la république dicte des lois,*" cried Merlin of Thionville, the Jacobin, in November, 1794. "*Bien conduite elle dictera encore des lois,*" prophesies Chateaubriand at Verona in 1822. Merlin and Chateaubriand ! Politically and temperamentally they are worlds apart. But for Frenchmen there is only one foreign policy. Only henceforth, if I may talk the jargon of psychology, for lack of practicable outlet the fundamental instinct of aggression is *repressed*. France suffered from a *neurosis*. And hence much of the abnormality of her political, as well as her diplomatic,history. From every government she demanded unvaryingly that the humiliation of the pact of Chaumont should be obliterated, that *la gloire* should return again. To exercise once more " the vigour which our glory demands " (a phrase of Lafitte's in 1828), this was her constant ambition.

Unhappily her rulers were never in a position to risk the *bouleversement* of Europe without which *la gloire* could not return to France. Chateaubriand would have

liked to risk the *bouleversement* in 1824—the glories of
Spanish intervention having been too much for his not
very stable mental balance. But Villèle and caution
prevailed. And even though the clear purpose of the
feudalist régime towards the close of the Bourbon
restoration had been to distract France by means of
glory from the resurrection of the *ancien régime* it had
very notably failed in the attempt ; and the handful
of students and workmen who initiated the Revolution
of 1830 were devotees of glory even more than of the
Republic. But the middle class deputies who assumed
control of the movement, and the middle class régime
which they established, were even more timid of the
bouleversement than the Bourbons. Popular agitation—
for intervention in Poland, for assistance to Mehemet
Ali—spent itself in vain against the prudence of Louis
Philippe. Louis Philippe remembered 1792, and knew
that his throne was not strong enough to survive war.
What did not occur to him was that it might not be
strong enough to survive peace either. And so—the
Revolution of contempt. The crowd which assembled
almost aimlessly in the Place de la Concorde on February
22nd, 1848, was animated no doubt by a great variety
of emotions ; but one emotion was shared by all its
elements : they were all contemptuous and all *bored*.
The July monarchy was not overthrown : it fell.

Second of the interwoven threads which make the
Revolution of 1848 is the Republican movement for the
logical completion of the revolutionary settlement by
the abolition of the compromise with monarchy ; the
residue, as I called it, of the aggressive force of the old
Revolution. The principal elements of this movement
are embodied in the policy of the official opposition in
the Chamber to which I have already referred, and I do

not wish to say much more of it. It seized upon the Revolution at its outset, but was immediately confronted with a new phenomenon.

It was confronted by the *third,* and vastly most important, of the contributory causes of the Revolution : the *new revolutionary idea.* We shall have to consider very carefully what exactly the new Revolution implied. The new movement is commonly distinguished as the *social,* from the *political,* Revolution. Even de Tocqueville thus defined it in a prophetic speech to the Chamber on January 29th, 1848, " *Ne voyez-vous pas que leurs passions, de politiques, sont devenues sociales* ? " " Their passions are no longer political but social." But all Revolutions, as I have observed, are social Revolutions. All Revolutions, that is to say, are due to social discomforts and set out to effect, ultimately, social changes. Thus the changes desired, and effected, by the Revolution of 1789, in spite of all the talk of contracts, were, as we have seen, social. It is true that hitherto it had been supposed that social changes could be effected by merely political formulæ. But this illusion survived longer in England than in France, for, during these years in which in France we trace the antecedents of the new Revolution, the English Revolutionaries, after a brief adherence to the Utopian Socialism of Robert Owen, produced nothing more inspired than the People's Charter, whose six points proposed, to cure the social miseries of the Industrial Revolution, such remedies as vote by ballot and equal electoral districts. In France, however, the Revolution no longer hoped to overcome the social evils, in which it still originated, by charters or contracts or any merely political device.

We do not need to look far into the Revolution of 1848 to detect the quality which distinguishes it from its predecessors. We need only take for example the curious anecdote with which de Tocqueville in his memoirs illumines transiently the unsearched obscurities of the popular feeling of the hour. A friend of his " had brought in from the country the daughter of a poor man whose difficulties had touched him, and had placed her in his household. On the evening of the first day of the insurrection he overheard this child remarking, as she cleared the table after dinner, ' Next Sunday '—and it was Thursday then—' it's us who'll be eating chickens' wings.' To which another small girl who worked in the house replied, ' Yes, and it's us who'll wear the fine silk dresses.' " It was, in fact, primarily at a redistribution of wealth that the new Revolution would aim. It was *the economic Revolution* : the Revolution of to-day. The people had realised that political change would not affect their discontents. " The people," observes de Tocqueville, " had at first attempted to better its lot by changing its political institutions . . . It was inevitable that sooner or later they should discover that what oppressed them was not the constitution but the immutable laws on which rests society itself ; and it was natural that they should be led to ask themselves if they had not the right and the power to alter these too, as they had the former."

The old Revolution had been directed against the feudal system, the new Revolution was directed against the industrial system. Now whereas the old revolutionary idea had grown through centuries, the new was actually expressed in action, within three decades of the establishment of the evil it was meant to uproot. So intolerable seemed the discomforts of the new industrialism. No wonder then that the body of theory behind the new Revolution was crude and immature.

A movement for the redistribution of wealth. Naturally

it did not appeal to the classes which had made, and profited by, the old Revolution. The middle classes had acquired Order and could obey Guizot's *Enrichissez-vous* undisturbed; the peasants had destroyed the feudal burden and owned their land. These were in fact the possessing classes, the heirs of the great legacy of 1789. But the artisan had gained from the Revolution precisely nothing. Indeed, it was only since the Revolution that the artisan had grown to be a ponderable factor in society. If he would modify industrial conditions he must make a Revolution of his own, of a new sort. Hence the radical difference in kind between the Revolution of 1848 and those before it—1789 had been a national movement; 1848 was the effort of a class—a class which had been left outside the national movement. Hence, too, the radical falsity of any view which conceals this gulf (such as that of those[1] who, believing all revolutionaries to be dupes of the same sinister force, have perforce to exaggerate the continuity of the Revolution). In fact the essential and abrupt distinction between the Revolution, whose last eruption is in 1830, and the Revolution whose first eruption is in 1848 is only obscured by the survival into 1848 (and, for that, into 1871) of what I have called the residue of the old Revolution, the surviving movement, that is, for its logical completion by the return of the Republic. But, as we shall see, what is dynamic and distinctive in the Revolution of 1848 belongs to the new, economic Revolution.

But before we come to the Revolution itself I must examine briefly that one of the interwoven threads of its antecedents between 1830 and 1848 which accounts for this distinctive character—the subterranean socialist propaganda of these years.

[1] *E.g.*, Mrs. Webster.

This strange efflorescence of " socialist " opinion may
be dated roughly from 1820, from about the time, that is,
of the Industrial Revolution in France, the problem of
which it proclaimed itself the solution. I speak of the
men who first spread these opinions as the first socialists,
although the label " socialist " is a little later than they,
and although its meaning is obscured by a score of various
interpretations. It is of little service to search very precisely for their intellectual ancestry. The French mind,
we know, is strangely credulous of abstract principles ;
an unprecedented evil, as these men had the merit of
perceiving, demanded heroic remedies ; and it is only
strange that, to meet the need, not more Utopias were
prescribed.[1] But at least we may differentiate two chief
types within the obscure socialist propaganda which first
forced itself upon the attention of Europe in 1848.
Thureau-Dangin in a noticeably hostile sketch of the
beginnings of French socialism has distinguished Leroux,
Buchez, and Fourier as successors of Saint-Simon from
Cabet, Louis Blanc, and Proudhon, whom he derives
more directly from Babœuf and the " Equals " of 1796.
But the distinction is based upon the accident that the
first three shared among them the dissolving discipleship
of Saint-Simon, and indeed the whole passage is pre-
judiced and uncritical.

In fact here clear-cut categories are impossible. Nor
need we delay to examine the work, strangely, and often
fantastically, individual, of most of these writers. In
two only the new revolutionary idea is presented so

---

[1] Mrs. Webster, inevitably, derives all socialists from Weishaupt, the arch-priest
of Illuminism. But she does this on the strength of such tenets as "Reason
should be the only code of man." " The end justifies the means." And if
these false but primeval commonplaces, ubiquitous throughout time, are
to be taken as evidence of parenthood, there is scarcely a doctrine or
writer in the world who may not be derived from Weishaupt, even those
who preceded him by many centuries.

luminously that no study of that idea can neglect them. The death of Saint-Simon, the greatest of these, preceded the Revolution of 1848 by twenty-three years, but in his work will be found almost every theory which has cut a figure in socialist propaganda throughout the century. The other, Louis Blanc, was journalist rather than thinker ; and popularised a formula which in 1848 he himself attempted to apply. Both of these are essential to our purpose.

The rest, though curiously interesting in themselves, concern us here chiefly as symptoms of the wide diffusion and variations of this great outcrop of confused thinking towards the always elusive remedy. But at least it should be observed that these are not anti-social conspirators (they have been so represented), but genuine, if often bewildered, idealists.

The only sinister figure, I think, among them is that of Fourier[1] whose barrack-lodged *phalanstères* of eighteen hundred souls with domesticities and work in common, even without his creed that the indulgence of the passions solves all problems, have a flavour which is evil as well as grotesque. Even so, Fourierism was not subversive. " It was not," says Lamartine, " a subversion of existing society, but a tremendous experiment in a regenerated society, demanding only, with respectful toleration of existing rights, discussion of its theories and opportunity for experiments."[2]

Proudhon[3] is at once more bitter, more solitary and more human. He hated society, but his hate is comprehensible ; for society had humiliated him since the days

---

[1] *Théorie des quatre mouvements*, 1808. *Association domestique et agricole*, 1822. *Nouveau monde industriel*, 1829.

[2] *Histoire de la Révolution de 1848*, i. 307.

[3] *Mémoire sur la propriété*, 1840.

when as a schoolboy he was punished for " forgetting "
the books he could not buy. " An immense anger," he
has been called, and his single contribution (so he
thought) to this perplexing universe was one phrase—
" Property is theft."
For the rest the lesser pre-runners of 1848 are at least
constructive enough to satisfy Saint-Simon's apothegm,
" *il faut un système pour remplacer un système.*"[1] And if
Cabet's *Voyage en Icarie* (1840) is little more than popular
Utopian (but communist) fiction, and if the mystic triads
in which Pierre Leroux[2] proposed to associate savant,
artist and artisan are less noteworthy than the rigid
state control which was to operate them, yet, memorably
enough, Buchez[3] preached Christian fraternity and sacrifice, a sort of co-operative Catholic socialism which proclaimed the duties of the people before its rights.
L'Atelier (1840-1850), inspired by him, was a journal
genuinely written and edited by working men. " The
Revolution," announced *l'Atelier*, should " proclaim
itself Christian, aim only at that which Christianity
enjoins." Thureau-Dangin is outraged at this " pre-
tended community of principle between the Gospel and
the Revolution," and, worse still, Buchez attached too
little importance to the authority of the Church.
These men, moreover, were experimentalists. A colony
of Cabet's communist Icarians survived thirty-nine years
(1849-1888), with varying fortunes, at Nauvoo, in Illinois.
Groups of workmen inspired by Buchez worked co-
operatively as well as publishing *l'Atelier*. And in 1832,
at Condé-sur-Vesgre, even Fourier's grim *phalanstère*
achieved a year of hideous life.

[1] Saint-Simon. *L'Organisateur. Œuvres,* vol. XX, p. 6.
[2] *De l'égalité* 1838.   *De l'humanité,* 1840.
[3] Died 1865. Flor. circ. 1840.

Such were the lesser protagonists in that twilit propaganda of whose audience before 1848 we know so little. Men who, perverse often and disingenuous, did yet feel keenly, and struggle to remedy, the spreading confusion and misery of the new underworld, which the prosperous middle class voters and place-seekers of the *pays légal*, though their views upon the authority of the Church were frequently all that could be desired, neglected altogether. Lamartine, their opponent in 1848, found in these men " a sincere and religious enthusiasm which raised masters and disciples alike above the evil thoughts, the miserable aims, and still more, the ferocity of spirit which have since been attributed to them." " They desired," he says, " a gradual and rational transformation, not a cataclysm. In these first hours of the explosion when the soul lays itself bare, no word of anger or vengeance passed their lips, no word which implied resentment or class-division . . . the members of the government most opposed to them in theory owe this testimony to history, to mankind and to God."[1]

Saint-Simon and Louis Blanc, the two greater figures in that secret drama, need closer consideration.

The high significance of Saint-Simon has not yet been recognised. The grotesque and worthless cult which exploited his name after his death in 1825 has obscured and discredited the real Saint-Simon and his teaching. But *Saint-Simonisme* has very little indeed to do with Saint-Simon : it was the negligible work of Enfantin and Bazard, and its pretentious immorality thoroughly earned the obloquy which had overtaken it by 1832. Saint-Simonism was a pseudo-religious cult, but Saint-Simon was a visionary critic of society, and his work lies at the roots of all subsequent socialist propaganda. And yet

[1] Lamartine : *Revolution de* 1848, i. 311, 313.

Thureau-Dangin[1] (for example), though he describes at length the childish pretensions of Enfantin and Bazard, all but completely ignores the writings of Saint-Simon himself. And a recent work,[2] on the strength of the meagre information supplied by Thureau-Dangin, even asserts that Saint-Simon " proclaimed the abolition of property . . . the destruction of civilisation."

It is unprofitable to attempt an intellectual genealogy for Saint-Simon. His prime quality is insight into the peculiar circumstances of his time, and if here and there through the texture of his generalisations show dimly the ghostly forms of the Utopians of all time—Plato and St. Augustine, Campanella and Sir Thomas More—yet his conclusions are necessarily both novel and his own. The principal works of Saint-Simon were *Du système industriel* (1821-2), *L'Organisateur* (1820), *Catéchisme industriel* (1823-4) and the *Nouveau Christianisme* (1824).[3] These titles in themselves suggest the significance of the man. For his remarkable achievement was that he first realised at the very outset of the Industrial Revolution that a new age had come to birth, and that to encounter its unprecedented problems much new thinking must be done. While, even twenty years later, the contented bankers and manufacturers of the July monarchy, so far from realising the need for hard thinking, were not so much as conscious that a new problem had come into being. The scientific and industrial age (as Saint-Simon put it) was visibly succeeding to the feudal and theocratic

[1] *Histoire de la Monarchie de Juillet*, vol. i, cap. 8.

[2] Mrs. Webster : *World Revolution*, p. 104. For this authoress, needless to say, Saint-Simon is a disciple of Weishaupt. " Saint-Simon, who we know " (she writes)" was connected with this formidable secret society (the Haute Vente Romaine), accordingly continues the great scheme of Weishaupt by proclaiming the destruction of civilisation."

[3] A bibliography will be found in Janet : *Saint-Simon et le Saint-Simonisme*. (Paris, 1878.)

and the manifest need of bewildered society was *organisation*. Saint-Simon was a constructive thinker. "*Il faut un système pour remplacer un système.*" The spirit of the eighteenth century had been critical, and the achievement of the eighteenth century had been the Revolution. But this work of destruction (for so he thought it) was transient and negative. And, in contrast, the spirit of the nineteenth century was to be the spirit of organisation and its work was to be construction. As he complains at the opening of the introduction to *l'Organisateur*[1] "The nineteenth century has not yet assumed the character which befits it ; it is still the character of the eighteenth which dominates the literature of thought. And this is why we are still in a state of revolution." "The exploitation of the universe by co-operation," such, according to Saint-Simon, is the goal of human activity in the new age of science and industry. "Every man should consider himself one of a band of hired workmen." The prophetic quality in all this is even more remarkable if we remember that the few years in which Saint-Simon's chief writings were published were those of the zenith of the Bourbon Restoration, during which the dominant party was so little conscious of the realities of the new world about it, that the only policy it could formulate was the resurrection of the feudal system *en bloc*. In his day Saint-Simon was all but solitary in his visionary realisation of new needs.

He did not propose to satisfy these needs by Revolution ; for Revolution, in his view, was an anachronism, belonging to the destructive age which had come to an end. "Progress," he observed, "is achieved in one of two ways, by revolution or dictatorship, and dictatorship is preferable to revolution." And accordingly it is

[1] *Œuvres*, vol. XX, p. 6.

to Louis XVIII that he appeals, in his *Lettre au roi*, to
place himself at the head of the industrial system ;
a singular echo of Mirabeau's advice to Louis XVI,
equally unheeding, that he should publicly accept the
Revolution of 1789 in its first stages. Louis XVIII was
to establish Saint-Simon's reforms by ordinance. In this
belief in authority Saint-Simon once more anticipates—
if in a different form—the socialism we know. Indeed
order is as much his object as it was the object of the
Revolution of 1789. "At present," he points out, " in
every activity it is the incapable who are charged with
the direction of the capable." But the order of which
Saint-Simon recognised the infinite need was order in
that new industrial world of which the Revolution of
1789 had not been so much as conscious.

Saint-Simon did not attack riches as such : indeed,
under the king, it is the principal bankers and industrial
magnates that he would place at the head of his new
industrial system. The *drones* whom he assails are those
who receive interest and do no work themselves ; and he
seems to make no exception in favour of those whose
income is the reward of their own past effort. Strangely
prophetic is Saint-Simon's recognition of the part to be
played in the new age by science. From his belief that
the goal of man is the exploitation of the world's re-
sources by co-operation he arrives at an altogether novel
conception of the nature of liberty. The direct object of
association is not liberty (as politicians just then repeated
more parrot-like than ever) : the object of association is
order. Liberty is in fact not an *end* nor even a means ; it
is a *result*—the result of man's progressive mastery of
nature. Man frees himself through science. And hence
the authority of the scientist in the society which Saint-
Simon forecasts, and the subaltern rôle of the mere

politician. Health, education, public works—everywhere authority is the expert's : the executive does but
supervise obedience to his enlightened direction.

Is it possible to overlook in this theory of progress
towards freedom, through organised and controlled
co-operation, its resemblance to the best known state-
ments of socialism in this country ? All the writings of
H. G. Wells (to take one example) testify to the vitality
and significance of Saint-Simon as the first socialist of
the new Revolution.

Thus far the work of Saint-Simon is not Utopian, or it
is Utopian only with the *Republic* of Plato ; that is, as
reviewing upon the ideal plane the forces latent in the
society which gave it birth. It is in fact an analysis,
continually astonishing in its penetration, of the implications of phenomena so novel that his contemporaries
had overlooked their very existence. And this is the
permanent claim of Saint-Simon upon history—a claim,
be it said, which has been overlooked. He does, however,
beyond this, sketch an artificial and ideal society ; the
picture indeed is presented in three phases: in *l'Industrie*,
in *l'Organisateur*, and in *le Système Industriel*. But this
imagined society with its grotesque particulars is often
as remote from reality as the most fantastic of the
Utopians, and I do not propose to discuss it here. The
achievement of Saint-Simon is independent of it.

It is impossible to estimate here the influence of Saint-
Simon upon his successors ; but it will be clear at least
that the principal features of his work recur constantly
throughout all later socialist thinking. This need not
mean that socialist propaganda was directly in debt to
Saint-Simon. At a time which made such demands upon
the sensitive imagination the same conceptions must
have been dimly present to many minds, and in the

history of ideas it can perhaps never be certain how far
the forerunner is symptom and how far cause. None the
less, and with every reservation made, Saint-Simon
remains of incontestable importance ; and there is no
doubt that to his insight the strangely early efflorescence
of French socialism is primarily due. We shall observe
the persistent vitality of his ideas when we examine, with
Louis Blanc, the socialist propaganda at one stage nearer,
as it were, to the new Revolution and our own day.

Louis Blanc had the mind and methods of a journalist,
and to this he owes his importance as a channel for the
revolutionary idea. Receptive rather than creative, his
work registers for us the ideas current in his time, and
as a vulgariser of ideas, rivalled only by Cabet, he was
to be largely responsible for the peculiar form taken by
the new Revolution in 1848.

Both *l'Organisation du travail* and *l'histoire de dix ans*
belong to 1840,[1] that *annus mirabilis* of the literature
of the new Revolution, which also saw the first publica-
tion of Proudhon's *Mémoire sur la propriété* and Cabet's
Voyage en Icarie as well as the *De l'humanité* of Pierre
Leroux and the journal *l'Atelier* inspired by Buchez.
The genealogy of a mind like Louis Blanc's is likely to be
far clearer than that of Saint-Simon. But his importance
is not his origin, but that, as populariser rather than
prophet, he crystallises for us the revolutionary idea on
the eve of the new Revolution. There is no doubt that,
like Cabet, he owed much to the communism of Babœuf,
which was reintroduced to France in 1828 by the *Histoire
de la Conspiration de Babœuf* of Buonarotti, who himself
had been of the Equals. Babœuf has hitherto been of

---

[1] Later editions of *L'Organisation du travail* state that it was originally printed
in 1839. This is probably an error. See Thureau-Dangin, *op. cit.*, vol. VI,
p. 119, note.

only negative significance to the revolutionary idea : for communism was alien to every phase of the Revolution of 1789, and indeed Babœuf himself was imprisoned by the Terror, and executed, unpitied, by the Directory. But by 1828 there were many who were ready to hail as Messianic any gospel which promised so thorough-going a remedy for the evils of the new industrialism, and, through Buonarotti, Babouvisme made great headway with the secret societies which from about 1830 were being converted to the new Revolution and particularly in the philosophic and debating clubs which under the auspices of Fourier or Cabet or Louis Blanc openly discussed the dogmas of socialism.

L'Organisation du travail is no more than a summary and handbook of the new ideas. The fourth edition of 1845, apart from answers to criticisms upon former editions, is a matter of only a hundred and two pages, of which eighty-four are devoted to a picture of the miseries of free competition and *laissez-faire*, and a mere eighteen to the remedies proposed by Louis Blanc. The book makes no pretences of being a scientific treatise : its manner indeed is unmistakable. It is journalism ; but, it has to be admitted, good journalism. The picture of French society in 1840 is an appeal to the heart at least as much as to the head. *The other day a child was frozen to death behind a sentry-box in the heart of Paris, and nobody was shocked or surprised at the event.* Such is the upshot of the opening sentence of *L'Organisation du travail*, and even to-day, in spite of three-quarters of a century of unhappy familiarity with its kind, the rest of the indictment remains moving and convincing. The writer is scarcely more angered by infant-murder and child-labour and by the vast degradation of the poor, everywhere expropriated and shunned, forced into crime

by society and hardened to crime by its prison system—
than by the half-contemptuous indifference of the rich.
" So great is the philanthropy of our legislature in
France," he writes, " that on one occasion the Chamber
of Peers went so far as to fix eight years as the earliest
age at which a child might have its personality destroyed
by entering the service of a machine." But the system
which countenances these dark things is not only evil,
it slowly commits suicide ; for the system of free competition bears within it the seeds of its own destruction.
And with journalistic *flair*—for the England of Palmerston
was bitterly unpopular in France—he makes England
his example of (what seems to him) the odious exaggera-
tion of free competition and *laissez faire.*

So much for Louis Blanc's sketch of the society he
knew, a society presided over by a minister whose
exhortation to it was " Grow rich ! " Thureau-Dangin
considers that the picture not only " perfidiously en-
venoms and exasperates the suffering," but " violently
exaggerates the disorder."

So much for the disease. Louis Blanc's remedies have
the brevity which is the soul, often of wit, but sometimes
of superficiality. In one word, communism is his pre-
scription or communism preceded by state socialism, the
communism of Buonarotti's *Conspiration de Babœuf* as
developed by twelve years of debate in the revolutionary
societies. For a comparison of *L'Organisation du travail*
with the fifteen articles of that *Analyse de la doctrine de
Babœuf* with which Paris had been placarded in the
year IV does not suggest that he owed much at first hand
to the leader of the Equals. Unlike Saint-Simon, Louis
Blanc looks forward to Revolution as well as reform ;
the necessary reform being too complex to be effected
without the transference of all power to the State. The

working classes are first to seize the State, then State-omnipotence, State-control of production, and State-creation—by means of a gigantic loan—of *ateliers sociaux*, " social workshops," which shall compete with and destroy the workshops owned by individuals : " using the weapon of competition to destroy competition " he calls this. Promotion in the *ateliers sociaux* after the first year is to be by election by the workpeople ; but rates of pay will be independent of promotion ; not according to capacity, but needs. Individuals are invited to lend their capital to the State, and the State will guarantee their interest ; but as to profits, they will be divided into three parts, one to form a fund for what we should call old age, sickness and unemployment benefits ; one to provide the instruments of production for new workers in the industry, which is to be open to all comers (it is clear that the author did not think out this feature of Utopia very clearly). The third part was to be shared equally among all members of the *atelier* : and soon, hoped Louis Blanc, their communist education would have progressed so far that they would wish to share equally their expenses as well as their receipts.

Such was the scheme of Louis Blanc. It is a little easy to forget that the theories which he crystallised and made popular grew unguided by the experience of practice and unpruned by adverse criticism and reached this maturity within two decades of the appearance of the evil which gave them birth. A wild and rapid growth ; small wonder that there was rankness in the increase. "A perilous and absurd chimera," Thureau-Dangin calls it. And Thureau-Dangin makes a good deal of Louis Blanc's ridiculously small stature, giving at length the story of his visit to Decazes, who mistook him for a boy, as well as Heine's facetious remarks upon *ce tribun imberbe*. The suggestion is partly that this was a man embittered by deformity, but partly that the physical insignificance has an intellectual counterpart, in view of which it would have been fairer to add Lamartine's picture of Louis Blanc in February, 1848. (Lamartine was an eyewitness of the scene, and politically an opponent.) " Among these groups the eye overlooked Louis Blanc, owing to the smallness of his stature. But he soon stood out from them, thanks to the sombre fire of his regard, the vigour of his gestures, the metallic ring of his voice and the vigorous determination of all his movements."

Perhaps Louis Blanc as writer and revolutionary did Europe no more than that least service indicated in a remarkable passage in his own introduction to his *Histoire de dix ans.* " What can we tell, after all ? Conceivably, if there is to be progress, all evil possibilities must first be exhausted. The life of humanity is long and the number of solutions conceivable is small. Every Revolution then is useful in this sense at least, that it absorbs one disastrous possibility." But even if Louis Blanc had done no more for Europe, for us at least, as students, he has crystallised the revolutionary idea as it must have been debated in many a workman's society in the Paris of the July monarchy.

Never have Utopians, or all-but-Utopians, nor so many of them, found such wide and immediate acceptance as these under the bourgeois régime. For never before had there been such pressing need of cure for so great and sudden an evil. What is more, the bourgeois oligarchy of the *pays légal* overlooked the campaign and the danger altogether : *there was no opposition* :[1] hence its persuasive

---

[1] To be exact, only that of M. Louis Reybaud's two volumes, *Études sur les reformateurs modernes.* See Thureau-Dangin, *op. cit.*, vol. 6, p. 145.

effect of being unanswerable. And, lastly, France of all countries was greediest of abstract principles.

A German, living in Paris at this time, was almost solitary in foreseeing the threat to constituted society. " Communism," wrote Heine, " is the sombre hero for whom is reserved a huge, if transient, rôle in the tragedy of our times : *and he is only waiting his cue to make his entrance on the stage.*"   On February 22nd a vast and not very purposeful crowd in the Place de la Concorde was crying *à bas Guizot*. By far the greater part of it had never heard of communism. But this was the cue.

CHAPTER VII

THE REVOLUTION OF 1848

I HAVE tried to disentangle and summarily to present the three constituents of the Revolution of 1848 : the universal dissatisfaction with the ingloriousness and corruption of the July monarchy ; the movement for the Republic as the logical completion of the first Revolution ; and, lastly, the new Revolutionary socialism. We shall find each playing its appointed part in the Revolution itself.

On the first day (February 22nd) the pervading discontent takes shape in vague disturbance which, on the second, defines itself as the successful insurrection against Guizot, his system and its results. This is the *first phase* (Feb. 22, 23).

The *second phase* is equally brief (Feb. 24-26). On the third day (February 24th) the Reform Party finds to its consternation that the Revolution is not over. The Republicans have taken it in hand. Louis Philippe abdicates ; a provisional government is acclaimed and proclaims the Republic.

The *third phase* is the struggle between the rival policies within the successful Republican party. On one side the Republicans-and-no-more for whom the Revolution had achieved its purpose when it proclaimed the Republic, the logical completion of the Revolution of

1789. The tricolour was their flag. On the other side those for whom the end of monarchy was no more than the inevitable preliminary to a profounder modification of society in the interests of the working man, the economic Revolution. Their emblem was the red flag. The struggle does not end until the Have-nots of the new Revolution are finally defeated by the Haves of the old in the bloody street fighting of June 24-26. Here—as the peasants pour in from the country to defend, together with their middle class co-heirs, the legacy of 1789— Paris is for the first time defeated by France, a fact of immense importance. At this point then the new Revolution is driven underground, to await further remarkable destinies.

Such was the Revolution of 1848 in brief. We will examine it in some detail, for invaluable to the students of revolutions is a revolution so compact, so brief, in many ways so typical. Moreover, among the contemporary records, besides the picturesque autobiographies, miscalled histories, of Louis Blanc and Lamartine, we possess in de Tocqueville's *Souvenirs* the evidence of an eye-witness of genius, himself the first and greatest student of revolutions.

First comes the Reform insurrection of February 22nd and 23rd. The political banquets, which the ministry of Guizot had forbidden, were the immediate occasion, but by no means the cause, of the Revolution. It was tacitly understood that the opposition would hold one last banquet, and that the government without obstructing it would charge its promoters in the courts, with whom the verdict would rest : that is all. On the 20th February almost all the opposition journals published an appeal to Paris at large to join in an immense demonstration on the day of the banquet ; the National Guard itself

was included in the invitation. The government at once
forbade the banquet, and announced that it would take
steps to prevent it by force. The 22nd was the appointed
day. There were crowds in the streets, uneasy but purposeless crowds which thronged past the Madeleine,
crossed that great central scene of so much bloodshedding
which Parisians have named the Place of Concord, and
so over the Pont Royale to the Chamber of Deputies.
There they were dispersed without loss of life by a
regiment of dragoons. De Tocqueville dined that night
with a fellow-deputy. Twenty places were laid, but only
five guests sat down to dinner. The five, he says, were
" pensive." On his way home he may have noticed the
distant flicker of the flames in which street-urchins were
burning some of the benches in the Champs Elysées.
Lamartine, at least, observed them thoughtfully.

At dawn, on the 23rd, troops occupied the principal
posts of vantage in Paris, and there awaited events,
extremely cold and uncomfortable. Few people were to
be seen about, only an occasional burst of distant firing
echoed mysteriously from the labyrinth of streets in the
neighbourhood of the Hotel de Ville. In the evening,
however, a large crowd encountered a regiment of the
line before the Ministry of Foreign Affairs, was fired on
by some misunderstanding, and took to its heels, leaving
a number of dead. Later that night the corpses were
placed on a bier and borne processionally by torchlight
through the streets. " The government is massacring
the people," sobbed de Tocqueville's cook next morning.
And through the night armed men went from house to
house, barricades were hastily put up, and the church
bells rang to summon Paris to further insurrection.
Louis Philippe could hear them distinctly from the
Tuileries. During that night he invited Thiers, leader of

the opposition, to form a government. The Reform-rebellion was over. Early in the morning of the twenty-fourth he lay down for a few hours, fully dressed. He could hear, where he lay, the confused murmur of conversation among his counsellors in an adjacent room, and beyond it the sounds of a distant but recurrent fusillade.

There had been an odd effect of discipline about the two columns which were the nucleus of the crowd which had got itself " massacred " this night of the twenty-third. They had seemed to be in no doubt about their objects or their route, these men, and to recognise officers from whom they received orders, and at least once a purposeful little band had detached itself from the main column and disappeared unostentatiously down a side street upon an unknown mission.

This nucleus was drawn, no doubt, from the secret societies which, in increasing numbers since 1830, had been giving shelter to illegal opinions. Louis Blanc gives an interesting picture, in the introduction to the *Histoire de dix ans*, of the French Carbonari under the Restoration drilling on straw in empty houses. The *Droits de l'homme*, the *Famille*, the *Saisons*—all preserved the republican and revolutionary traditions, and, as we have seen, to these since 1830 had been adding itself the new revolutionary economic gospel. The secret societies were often divided into sections of twenty members, each with an officer and under-officer. (Thus, for example, the *Droits de l'homme*.) And hence no doubt the all but military discipline in portions of the crowds of 1848. All these societies, too, had had experience in one or other of the insurrections of 1832, 1834, and 1839. But it must be recognised that it was these societies which were created by the requirements of forbidden revolutionary opinion, not the opinion which was created by the societies. Nor must the importance of the secret societies even in this merely Parisian Revolution be exaggerated.[1] Lamartine, who was in as good a position as anyone to estimate their influence, observed that " the very limited effects which can be produced by a conspirator . . . are influential only when they serve a general idea or a pre-existing passion . . . In the modern state the only all-powerful conspirator is public opinion."

This insurrection of the twenty-second and twenty-third had been the work of the party of reform ; *à bas Guizot* had been its rallying-cry. It had been successful, and there had even been illuminations at night. The second insurrection developed out of it early on the twenty-fourth. The troops proved reluctant to take the offensive against it, and Thiers ordered them to withdraw on the Tuileries and sent his colleague—Barrot—to announce to the crowds the concessions extorted from the king. He himself within a few hours was to be slinking homewards *incognito* and by devious routes, shaken by hysterical sobs, muttering incoherently to himself and incontinently turning tail at the first hint of a crowd—even of street-urchins. The Palais-Royal, original home of the house of Orleans, was captured and pillaged. Louis Philippe, attempting to rouse the enthusiasm of the National Guard, was received with chilling indifference, lost heart and abdicated in favour of the Comte de Paris, his grandson. That afternoon the crowd destroyed the throne in the Tuileries. The Chamber of Deputies, which had proclaimed the Comte de Paris king and his mother regent, was invaded, the Republic

[1] For Mrs. Webster all revolutions and revolutionary opinions are artificially manufactured by secret societies, and even within the secret societies the members are mostly " dupes " of highly mysterious forces which propagate revolutionary opinion among them as a means to their own ulterior end, which is vaguely described as "the destruction of civilisation."

was proclaimed and the republican members of the
Chamber announced amidst uproar the members of a
provisional government selected by the staff of the
National Guard. These made their way across the tumult
of Paris to the Hotel de Ville, where they had to effect
a sort of coalition with the government already selected
by the *Reforme.*

On the twenty-sixth the Provisional Coalition Government proclaimed the Republic. Once more France was
to receive a Revolution ready made from Paris. The
Provisional Government had indeed some misgivings in
this matter ; its first draft of the proclamation stated
that *neither the people of Paris nor the Provisional
Government pretend to substitute their opinion for the
opinion of the citizens, who will be consulted as to the final
form of the Government.* Lamartine asserts that in one of
his many addresses to the mob in the streets at this time,
speaking of the proposed Republic, he said, " We have
only one right, that of proclaiming . . . our own will,
as the people of Paris . . . leaving to the country and
its thirty-six millions who are not present and have the
same right as ourselves . . . the expression of their
sovereign will by means of universal suffrage . . . the
one foundation of any national republic." The people
shouted in reply, " Yes, yes. France is not here. Paris
is the head, but Paris must guide, and not tyrannise over,
the body." Thus remote was the populace for the moment
from the Jacobin view of the relation of Paris to France.
A later draft of the proclamation was less apologetic :
*The Provisional Government wills the Republic, under con-
dition of approval by the people, who will be immediately
consulted.* And in the final announcement of the 26th
the Provisional Government appeared to have overcome
its scruples : *In the name of the French people, Monarchy,*

under every form, is abolished without possibility of return.
Without possibility of return ! Thus had the men of
1789 abolished the Bourbon monarchy and the restored
Bourbon monarchy the empire of Napoleon.

The Provisional Government had now achieved the
only task on which it was agreed. It had no recognisable
mandate, no instruments save what it could improvise
and no authority save what it could usurp. And from
now onwards it carried disruption in its heart.

The third, last, and longest phase of the Revolution is
occupied by the conflict between the warring principles
within the Provisional and Coalition Government. The
issue between them is clear. The Republicans of the old
Revolution (Lamartine and five others) were for the
Republic, the democracy of universal suffrage and no
more. The new revolutionaries (Louis Blanc, Albert,
Flocon) were for carrying out the further, economic
Revolution, without waiting for the verdict of the nation.
The instincts of Jacobinism were reviving rapidly indeed.
And at the moment the new revolutionaries wielded the
same formidable weapon as the men of 1793, an armed
body of supporters in the streets, organised, not now in
the Jacobin clubs, but in the *Société républicaine centrale*
of Blanqui and the *Club de la Révolution* of Barbès. For
some days no soldiers, no police were to be seen about
the streets ; " the people alone carried arms, kept watch
over public places, was on guard, issued orders, and
awarded punishments."

But in spite of this resumption of tradition there is a
new and quite unmistakable tang of modernity about
this Revolution. Thus de Tocqueville observed " a very
general effort to placate the new master. Great landowners liked to recall that they had always been hostile
to the bourgeois class and favourable to the people : and

the bourgeois themselves remembered with a certain pride how their fathers had been workmen, and when, owing to the inevitable obscurity of genealogies, they could not trace themselves back to a workman who had actually worked with his hands, they would at least attempt to descend from a ne'er-do-well who had made his fortune for himself. In fact the desire for the publicity of such details was as great as a little while ago it would have been for their concealment." And " just now everyone did his best to make what he could out of any black sheep the family possessed. Any cousin, or brother or son one might be lucky enough to own who had ruined himself by his excesses was well on the way to succeed ; while if he had contrived to win notoriety by some extravagant theory or other there was no height to which he might not aspire. The majority of the commissaries and sub-commissaries of the government were persons of this sort." The Duc de Broglie, poor gentleman, daily expected the collapse of civilisation.

The clubs began to establish their dictatorship at once. Even on February 25th an armed workman, spokesman of an immense crowd, demanded the *right to work* (*droit au travail*), Louis Blanc's phrase. Next day the establishment of *national workshops* was decreed.

On February 28th another organised demonstration demanded a Ministry of Progress. It carried banners on which were the words *Organisation du travail*, a phrase again of Louis Blanc's, and Louis Blanc himself supported the demand, and succeeded in persuading the government to create a Workers' Commission. Louis Blanc and Albert took up their quarters in the Luxemburg, whither they summoned representatives of various trades. And there this Commission decreed the reduction of the working day from eleven to ten hours in Paris, from twelve to eleven in the provinces. Such were the not very formidable first-fruits of Louis Blanc's " perilous chimera." The employers, however, paid remarkably little attention to the modest manifesto, and the Luxemburg Commission, which was permitted neither authority nor money, could scarcely enforce it.

For the third time, on March 17th, the clubs organised a *journée*; this time to exact the postponement for a fortnight of the election of the Assembly which was to supersede the Provisional Government. In this singularly short interval the country was to be converted to socialism. For the third time, and the last, the clubs were successful. On this occasion Blanqui (director of the *Société républicaine centrale*) was spokesman. " His speech amounted," says Lamartine, " to a demand for the implicit obedience of the government to the dictatorship of the mob as expressed by the clubs." For Jacobinism, in fact.

On April 16th there was yet another effort, and it failed : the bourgeois members of the National Guard lined up before the Hotel de Ville with cries of " Down with the communists ! " The clubs had more than half Paris against them and the whole of France.

Meanwhile the government was experimenting with " national workshops." These were not organised by Louis Blanc, neither did they resemble the " social workshops " suggested in *L'Organisation du Travail*. The members did not work at their own craft, but were regimented into brigades which were set to level the Champs de Mars at two francs a day (and, later, one franc when there was no work), a system ruinous to the exchequer and humiliating to the worker. Unemployment growing continually, the numbers in the *ateliers nationaux* rose from 6,000 in March to 100,000 in May ; many of them were artists, actors, men of letters, clerks and the like. The government, which was responsible for their distress, was in fact distributing charitable relief under a not very convincing disguise. The *ateliers nationaux*, thinks Lamartine, were a guarantee against disorder and socialism. " They counterbalanced," he says, " the Luxemburg commission and the clubs, and on several occasions saved Paris, though Paris did not know." They became " seditious " themselves only with the arrival of the Assembly in Paris and its plan for their own dissolution. Clearly this was an expedient, not a system ; and clearly the *ateliers nationaux* (where, whatever their own skilled craft, men worked all together at the same unskilled labour) were notably unlike the *ateliers sociaux* of Louis Blanc, to whom a remarkable historical perversion has sometimes attributed them. " Directed and controlled by leaders who shared the secret views of the anti-socialist members of the government," says Lamartine of the experiment of 1848, " they were instinct with the spirit of Louis Blanc's adversaries." The failures of 1848 are no reflection upon socialist theory, for the socialists were never in control even of the Provisional Government, and with the advent of the Constituent Assembly elected by universal suffrage they became impotent.

The Assembly met on May 4th. Universal suffrage had given an overwhelming majority to the possessing classes, and in an overwhelming majority the Assembly approved the anti-socialist Republic. Only one or two of the new revolutionaries sat in the Assembly, and the executive commission of five which it appointed and which was to name the ministers was hostile to them. The clubs remained the stronghold of the new Revolution. It was clear that there would soon be conflict once again, and perhaps mortal conflict, between this Paris of the clubs and France. In 1793 we saw Paris dictatress of a powerless and not very resentful France. In 1830 too, although a group of provincial deputies speedily assumed control of it, the Revolution was Paris-made. But in 1848 France was becoming consciously restive beneath the yoke of her feverish capital.

De Tocqueville, in his provincial constituency, at the time of the elections for the Constituent Assembly of 1848, observed this new impatience at close quarters. " For the first time," he says, " Paris inspired universal hatred as well as universal terror. In France the attitude of the provincials towards Paris and the central authority of which it is the seat is very much like that of the English towards their aristocracy, which they view sometimes with impatience and often with jealousy, but which in their hearts they love because they always hope to employ its privileges for their own ends. Now, however, Paris and those who spoke in her name had so misused their power and seemed to take the rest of the country into so little account, that the idea of shaking off the yoke and at last achieving independence presented itself to many minds which had never dreamt of such a thing before."

And in 1848 France was an altogether more formidable rival than in 1793 or 1830. The extension of the telegraph was beginning to make her *aware*. The violent decisions of Paris no longer came to her belated and irreparable : she was growing into an organic and self-conscious whole. But if the telegraph had given her consciousness, the more recent development of the railway had given her *power*. The deputies who upheld her majesty would no longer be left defenceless to the street insurrections of Paris. When de Tocqueville set out for Paris his constituents bade him farewell with tears in their eyes, " for it was generally believed in the provinces that the deputies would be exposed to great danger in Paris, and several of the good folk said to me, ' If the National Assembly is attacked we will come and defend you.' "

And lastly, besides being more conscious and more formidable, the provinces had in 1848 a very particular quarrel with their capital. As we have seen, in Paris in 1848 a violent minority once more attempted to impose its will upon the country ; and this will was not, as in 1793, the national will for victory concentrated in a class but the will of a class for its own advancement. This class, as we saw, found no place in a society which had been remoulded and had hardened into its new shape before the existence in it of a new element had been suspected. Not participating in the legacy of the Revolution of 1789, that class desired a Revolution of its own, the economic Revolution of the Have-nots against the Haves : of the excluded, against the heirs, of 1789. Unfortunately for the new revolutionaries the land settlement of the old Revolution, by parcelling out the soil of France in infinite sub-division, had included among the possessing class the vast majority of the nation ; and though these peasants owned little, those who own least are usually the most tenacious of their property. Hence the sinister news of the designs upon property did not, like English Chartism, alarm the middle classes only, but united provincial France in one compact brotherhood against the half of Paris. Here and there in the towns the indus- trial workers espoused the new Revolution. But France outside her cities was of one mind : in face of the threat to property all classes and parties drew instinctively

together. " Property . . . had become a sort of brotherhood., Rich . . . and poor . . . all held themselves
brothers and all were equally concerned to defend the
common heritage." Such was the mind of provincial
France on May 4th at the time of the meeting of the
National Constituent Assembly, to which it had returned
so great a majority against the new Revolution. In less
than two months it was to be at death grips with the
new principle in the streets of Paris.

During those few intervening weeks Paris saw again
the tactics of Jacobinism. It was argued daily in the
clubs, notes de Tocqueville, that " the people is always
superior to its delegates, and never completely resigns
its will into their hands. A principle true enough, from
which, however, was drawn the false consequence that
the workmen of Paris *were* the people of France." This
was the principle put into practice upon May 15th, when
an immense crowd invaded the Assembly, and amidst
uproar and confusion declared the Assembly dissolved
and proclaimed a Socialist Provisional Government. The
National Guard arrived not a moment too soon and dispersed the demonstrators in inglorious flight. De Tocqueville's recollections of the whole amazing scene should be
studied carefully by anyone interested in the psychology
of crowds.

Six days later was held a Feast of Concord ; a mani-
festation of fraternity at which three hundred thousand
armed men, carrying the rifles with which they were to
shoot each other down next month, defiled past a platform on which were seated the members of the National
Assembly each with a pistol, a life-preserver, or a dagger
concealed about his person. The official programme en-
joined " fraternal confusion," and the confusion at least
was unmistakable.

By now civil war was in the air. Sooner or later Haves
and Have-nots must come to grips. And inevitably it
was upon the *ateliers nationaux* that the issue was
joined. The Assembly was determined to dissolve this
vast camp of over a hundred thousand armed and
discontented workmen. These were still employed,
humiliatingly and unproductively, upon levelling the
Champ de Mars. " It is not our will to work that is
lacking," they protested, " but useful work suited to our
callings " ; and they refused to disband. Fighting began
on June 24th. The workmen fought without leaders, but
with the utmost resolution. Never before or since have
they struggled with such good hope. For a victory in
Paris might give them France, and the socialist theories
being in their heyday still it seemed to them that victory
would be followed by the millennium. But the very
ferocity of the insurrection was fatal to it : for the
possessing classes could not help but realise that either
it must be crushed, or the society they knew destroyed.
And consequently they, too, left their houses and fought
desperately. For both sides it was victory or slavery.

And for the first time France intervened. Already on
the 25th by every road not actually held by insurgents,
the possessing classes, noble and peasant alike, were
pouring into Paris. By the 26th they were coming from
five hundred miles away ; and while the insurgents had
no reserves, the defence could draw upon the whole of
France. France had defeated Paris, and this defeat
profoundly modified the form taken by the revolutionary
idea when it next emerged, in the Commune of 1871.
For the first time the whole was able to impose its will
upon the part : a fact of tremendous significance.
Perhaps never again—consider this—will a minority
carry a revolution to success, at least by way of

insurrection. In this year a page is turned in the history of revolutions, *and conceivably the last*.

In this conflict one bond had held together the defence, one interest it shared in common—property. An aged kinsman of de Tocqueville's refused to leave the fighting. " What would these brave folk say if I left them ? " he replied, pointing to his heterogeneous comrades in arms. " They know that I have much more to lose than they if the insurrection triumphs." By the 26th the victory had been won. Of the prisoners the majority were shot out of hand or transported *en masse* without trial. In less than six months Louis Napoleon was Prince President of the Republic.

The new and short-lived constitution of 1848 had asserted, together with the classic dogma of the separation of powers, that " all power emanates from the people." The legislature was an assembly of 750 elected by universal suffrage (for the first time the Revolution was completely justifying the Declaration of Rights of 1789) ; the executive was a President to hold office for four years, choosing his own ministers. Who was to elect the President ? If the Assembly, it would elect Cavaignac. But if the people ? Lamartine knew that he would not be elected by the Assembly. " Let God and the people pronounce," he said. " Something must be left to Providence." God and the people, he hoped, would pronounce in favour of himself. By December, 1848, however, the people at least had decided for a man with unusually short legs and a face like a fish. Once more the Revolution was about to hand itself over to a despot.

It is instructive to note, in this matter of electing the President, the completely divergent wills of the people and their representatives. By orthodox theory the will of the Assembly was the will of France, and the Assembly would have chosen Cavaignac. Twice already, however, in 1793 as well as in 1848, we have seen the Paris streets claiming to speak for France : they would have chosen Ledru-Rollin. And France did in fact choose Louis Napoleon. Each of the three " Frances " would have spoken differently . The truth is that the Assembly had been elected for a definite purpose, to protect the principle of property against Paris, and, this duty once discharged, its will bore no relation to the will of its constituents. This was in Louis Napoleon's mind when, preluding despotism, he invited its successor, the Legislature, to " associate itself with the national will of which his own election had been the expression." This justification he had too for the appeal by plebiscite to France. Since, however, the plebiscite was preceded by a bloody and treacherous *coup d'état*, and accompanied by about ten thousand transportations, the justification was morally of the slenderest.

Plebiscite accepted both the *coup d'état* of December, 1851, and the assumption of the imperial title a year later (December, 1852). For a second time the Revolution of 1789 had surrendered to Cæsar. And in return for what ? The first Empire, we have seen, while destroying the form, preserved the substance of the first Revolution ; and the second Empire too, while destroying the form, undertook to preserve the essentials of the substance. The distinction is that the first Napoleon was needed to guarantee and protect the achievement of a vast movement of the human spirit in its creative phase ; the second Napoleon came to defend in a movement static now and not creative that part of its achievement which it could not be cajoled into bartering away. The first was a task for genius, the second for cunning.

But if Louis Napoleon stood for the preservation of the old Revolution he stood for the destruction of the new. In the eyes of the middle classes and peasants he guaranteed property against the *Rouges* who, after the disaster of 1848, were believed to be plotting a second rising for 1852. Once more Empire was welcomed because it promised *Order*. And if the name Napoleon spelt Order it spelt *Glory* too. Of the hundreds of thousands of peasants who voted for that name not a few supposed themselves to be voting for the " Little Corporal " himself. After more than three decades in which to weary of weakness and humiliation, France was heartsick for the Napoleonic touch. Glory, as we saw, had been the one desire common to all parties in the Revolution of 1848 : Order had become an even more urgent need in face of the threat of the new revolutionaries to society as constituted by the old. In return for security for these two chief elements in the substance of the old revolution, France was prepared to forego the third, Equality, and, a little less readily, since the loss was more apparent and immediate, the form, the Republic. Thus it was the New Revolution which yielded to Louis Napoleon, and this was the element in the Revolution of 1848 which failed. The old Revolution welcomed him as protector of its tradition, and the Revolution of 1848 in so far as it desired no more than Glory, and then Order, may be said to have succeeded. And thus Napoleon the third, like Napoleon the first, was demanded by the needs of a Revolution ; he was less urgently demanded, less the inevitable, because the forces which called for him were spent.

The nature then of the appeal of Bonapartism was constant. But it is interesting to note that neither the first Napoleon nor his nephew had foreseen that this would be so. The uncle had employed the unwonted leisure of St. Helena in remoulding the tradition, in the interests of the hoped-for successor, nearer what he supposed to be the heart's desire of France. For France in 1815 might easily be mistaken for a country weary of the rigours of Order and the perils of Glory ; (he was an indifferent psychologist) ; and the nephew did his best to perpetuate the revised tradition in his *Des Idées Napoléoniennes,* published in 1839. It was asserted by this carefully considered reinterpretation that the Empire was always to have become Liberal, as, by force of circumstance, it had shown some signs of becoming in the *Acte Additionel* of the Hundred Days, when France was to have been educated up to freedom if Waterloo had not intervened. The Empire stood in fact for Liberty and not for Order. Also that only England had frustrated Napoleon's real desire for peace and a United States of Europe. The Empire meant not Glory but universal peace. It is interesting, in view of this laborious perversion of the truth, to reflect that it was quite unnecessary, since although in 1851 France accepted Napoleon III because his " name was a programme in itself," what hypnotised her was, as we have seen, precisely the legend in its original, unaltered version. Glory and Order ! Such were the demands of all France save the Socialists. Could Louis Napoleon satisfy them ? Upon the answer to that question depended the fortunes of the revolutionary idea. For the new Revolution, unlike that of 1789, was not powerful enough by itself to destroy a government. It could but hope to rush in once more, as in 1848, to fill the void when government had been overthrown by other and more widely disseminated discontents.

CHAPTER VIII

THE LAST REVOLUTION
(1852-1871)

A HISTORY of the fortunes of the revolutionary idea in 1848, as before 1830, would in itself be all but the political history of France. But after 1851 the Revolution is once more driven underground, and its history, where it has one, becomes once more infinitely remote from that of France.

The official political history of France is soon told. France was frozen by a despotism, which she tolerated for a while in the knowledge that the despot would protect Property and the hope that he would achieve Glory. Perhaps in 1856, when Paris, for the Congress after the Crimean War, was once more the political capital of Europe, it seemed for a brief moment as if Glory might have returned to stay. If Glory had returned, the Empire might be ruling France to-day : there is scarcely any price France would not pay for Glory. But by 1867 the last tragic act of the Mexican tragi-comedy had made it clear that Glory could never again be hoped for from the dull-eyed invalid in the Tuileries.. The increasingly representative institutions of the liberalising Empire of 1869 were an attempt to share the responsibilities of dishonour with a nation which would have been invited to an exceedingly small part in the credit for Glory. And in 1870 the second Empire was swept neck and crop, iron and pasteboard alike, into the gulf of Sedan. If any two errors in particular can be said to have been the destruction of a system which was pasteboard from the first these were errors of foreign policy, both of them ; the illusion of nationality, which permitted and indeed abetted the growth of powerful nation-states, not Italy only, but Prussia ; and the disastrous policy of compromise between Liberal and Catholic in the treatment of Italy and the Pope. Louis Napoleon was once persuading his small son to recite one of his fables : the child professed that he had forgotten the end of them all. " Then tell us the beginning of one of them." " I have forgotten the beginning." " Then let us have the middle," suggested the Emperor. " *Mais, papa,*" replied the unfortunate child, " *où commence un milieu* ? " Napoleon III was the last person in the world of whom to ask " Where a middle begins." The innocent question epitomises the whole fatality of the second Empire.

As he frequently announced, Louis Napoleon represented the will of the people ; and in order to sustain his rôle conscientiously he was at pains to obliterate that will when it was hostile to himself. He was not content with the transportations and exiles of the *coup d'état,* nor was it only the republicans and revolutionaries (in prison, transported, or plotting uselessly in the cafés of Brussels and London) that he silenced. Thus a woman was arrested at Tours for saying that the vine-disease was going to break out again, the prefect on her release threatening her with perpetual imprisonment if she persisted in spreading bad news. At the elections the government presented its own official candidates, paid their expenses, and enlisted all its servants in their support. Election meetings were forbidden, and the election was managed by the mayor (appointed by the government). At the end of the first of the two days' voting, the mayor, whose advancement depended upon the success of the official candidate, would take the voting urn home with him. It is only surprising that under these conditions the government ever lost an election. And, needless to say, the revolutionary idea found no legitimate channel of expression. The only journal permitted to the opponents of the Empire was the *Siècle*,[1] and the *Siècle*—it was the last touch to a system half ghoulish, half comic-opera—was controlled by the Emperor.

Such was the official political history of the reign, and these were the reasons for the creation of a void in 1870 which first the orthodox Republic and then the so-called Communards rushed in to fill. As under the monarchy of July, there are, broadly speaking, three sorts of revolutionary. First, the orthodox republicans, relicts of the Revolution of 1789 ; then the socialist partisans of the new Revolution, many of them becoming Communists under the grim influence of Marx ; and lastly, distinguishable from these but essentially unimportant, those sinister and unhappy figures of the underworld who desired violence for its own sake, members of secret societies often, personified rather than led by Blanqui, certain to emerge into horrible notoriety in the course of a Revolution, which, whatever its nature, they would welcome but could never bring about, and as certain to relapse into their proper obscurity as soon as order of any kind began to be restored.

---

[1] De la Gorce's account of the *Siècle* (*Histoire du Second Empire*, 3rd edn., ii. 81-84) is worth reading if only as a piece of rich and partially unconscious comedy.

Although only the policy of the first of these types can strictly be called Jacobin, the distinctive Jacobin claim for the dictatorship of a minority might be advanced by any of them. It is with the revolutionary idea among the socialists of the new Revolution that we are principally concerned, and its history is sharply cut in two, for whereas under the July monarchy the growth of the new revolutionary idea, equally remote from the official politics of the reign, was fully embodied in the Revolution of 1848, the modification of revolutionary thought under the second Empire finds no direct expression in the confused doings of 1871. The influence at work during the later years of the Empire is that of Karl Marx and the so-called Workers' International, but the theory behind the Revolution of Paris in 1871 is the theory of the Commune. Now the theory of the Commune is directly associated with the whole of the evolving idea we have traced since 1789 ; for it is the theory forced upon Paris by the victory of France over her in 1848 and the prospect of that victory being repeated in 1871. Jacobinism having been defeated in 1848, the Commune was the form taken by the will of Paris to dominate France, and thus the Commune and its defeat is the natural last act of the intellectual drama of which we are spectators. There perhaps for Western Europe the transient phenomenon of Revolution ends. The philosophy of Marx, on the contrary, and the economic theories of the International, although chronologically they fall within this period, are yet very little related to the development we have been tracing, being rather the germ of events which lie beyond our period altogether. For our purpose what is important about Marx is not his influence upon the history of France, but the influence of the history of France upon him.

This is indeed an aspect of Marx which is of great significance and has been neglected. The part played by Marx in French affairs can be described briefly. For the German edition of the *Communist Manifesto* was published in 1848, only a few days before the Revolution, and was scarcely known to the revolutionaries of that year; but the Provisional Government invited Marx, who had just been banished from Brussels, to Paris. "A free France," they said, " opens her gates to you." Marx, mistaking the Revolution for the ultimate conflict of his anticipation, betook himself to Paris and thence to Cologne, where as editor of the *Neue Rheinische Zeitung* he published his heartless advice for " abridging the hideous death agonies of society." In 1849 he returned to Paris, but though his hosts were still free it was seemingly with a different brand of freedom, and they banished him to a distant corner of Brittany, whence he soon crossed to London. Here he began to work at *Capital* and here he presided over the birth of the International.

The idea of this society was conceived in 1862, when a deputation of French workmen visiting the International Exhibition in London foregathered with some English workmen who advocated " the union of labourers among themselves." The exchange of ideas, and perhaps assistance, however, not socialism in any form, was their object. In 1864 the " International Association " sprang from these origins : " The economical emancipation of Labour " was its " great aim," but, once more, no particular organisation of society is demanded. Under the influence of Marx, however, the Congresses of the International adopted the main features of the socialism of the *Communist Manifesto* ; and in the last years of the second Empire the International became a centre

for revolutionary propaganda in France. The vaguer
and more idealist French socialism of 1848 was hardening
into the German drill-sergeant system of Marx. And yet,
as we shall see, such theory as the confused insurrection
of 1871 had time to commit itself to was distinctively
French, and save for one or two not very important
particular measures, the Commune owed nothing at all
to Marx. Indeed, of the seventy-eight members of its
Conseil général only about twenty were members of the
International. Accordingly, it will not be necessary to
concern ourselves at length with more than one of the
five chief theories of Marx.

Historically, in the materialistic interpretation of
history—economically, in its theory of value and its
prophetic law of the concentration of capital—and philosophically, for a view of human nature so childishly
mechanical that it out-Benthams Bentham himself, the
system of Marx has been proved false times out of
number.[1] Indeed, it is *fundamentally* false : for it is
certainly true that society will never be regenerated as
long as its main purpose is the accumulation of wealth,
or until its acquisitive impulses are transcended by the
creative instincts and things spiritual become more
precious to it than things material ; that is to say, until
the economic motive, which for Marx dominates human
nature and human history, is consigned to its proper
insignificance.

Anyone familiar with the enduring reputation of Marx
must be astonished at the limitations of the achievement
which earned it. The truth is that Marx lives in his fifth
doctrine, the prophecy of the inevitable success of the
coming revolution of the proletariat ; and this has

[1] H. J. Laski's essay on Marx (pub. Fabian Society, 1s.) is an admirable short
summary and critique.

worked rather as a psychological process of suggestion than a reasoned theory. Conflict and victory, he says, are alike inevitable ; " Capitalism produces its own gravedigger." Communists have only two functions : to prepare for the Revolution—by forming their own secret armed force—and to consolidate it when it has come, by means of a despotic dictatorship : once more the Terror is to be wielded by a minority ; for the end justifies the means ; democracy, freedom, and majority-rule are alike illusions, and communists, who will always be in a minority, cannot afford to wait for the consent of the people. Indeed, it would follow from Marx' doctrine that revolution is justified in any cause in which the shedders of blood happen to believe profoundly. Liberty and equality mattered little to Marx, the Prussian. But if it is the chief defect of the form of society he attacked that it denies liberty and equality to the mass of working people it must be said that all Marx' theories offer in exchange is a bloody and prolonged revolution which, if successful, would perpetuate in an acuter form the principal vices of the society it proposes to destroy.

Beyond this dictatorship of a violent minority Marx did not look far. Once the régime of class distinction and individual rights was destroyed the era of equality, he thought, would succeed to it as soon as a new psychology had been created by the intermediate dictatorship. It is in this doctrine (and it is prophecy rather than doctrine) that Marx lives. He contrived by the very confidence of his assertion to permeate revolutionary socialism with his own belief in the inevitability of the final catastrophe of Capitalism ; and to-day thousands who are altogether ignorant of the reasoning upon which that prophecy was based are convinced that Marx has proved the necessary success of the always approaching revolution. Marx'

Capital has been called the bible of the working man, but working men have never been familiar with its chapter and verse ; only with the hope it sanctions of a dreadful emancipation to come. And theorists who are bitterly opposed to every other feature in his doctrine yet acclaim Marx as a major prophet merely because he did prophesy. Thus the revolutionary Sorel, who approves little socialist dogma, approves Marx because he kept constantly before the eyes of the proletariat the vague but constant ideal of revolution which he himself has transmuted into the mystic doctrine of the general strike.[1]

Marx was a Prussian Jew. He loved little and he hated enormously—his fellow-socialists most of all. His whole life was hatred ; and this alone, even if there had been no error in his thought, condemns his system to futility. For the salvation of mankind will never come out of hate. This is a profound truth, and it invalidates a good deal more than half of the revolutionary gospels. Marx' revolutionary civil war and its ensuing Terror, for example, must inevitably breed, as experience has taught our generation, precisely those passions which must be fatal to any system of equality or brotherhood such as he proposes to set up. The destruction, however, of the existing order was perhaps for Marx more essential even than the establishment of the new.

It was his profound faith in the certainty of the ultimate Communist Revolution which has given Marx his power over Europe. What gave Marx this confidence ? Undoubtedly the history of France. He read there of a violent minority seizing, remodelling and controlling the government of France in 1793. Indeed, in 1793, it might even claim to have justified its usurpation. In 1830 once more a minority presented a new government to an

[1] Sorel : *Reflexions sur la Violence.*

uncomplaining France. And in 1848 Marx himself had
seen France for some while ruled by half Paris. Even
1871 did not shake his confidence. Once more half Paris,
or less than half of it, claimed to dictate the constitution
of France. It did not succeed, but it might, he thought,
have succeeded. Better fortune, a little more determination . . . A few barricades, a day or two of firing, so it
seemed, and even a thousand or so of revolutionaries
(provided they were disciplined to the standards of a
Prussian) could impose their vision of social regeneration
upon their millions of fellow-countrymen.

So it seemed. But how much Marx overlooked, or did
not know ! He forgot that no longer even in France was
the stampeding of the administration in Paris enough to
overawe the country permanently ; though the days of
June, 1848, were themselves enough to prove it. He did
not realise that in the modern state the arming and
disciplined training of a revolutionary minority, even of
a few thousands, would become increasingly impossible.
Nor that, even if it were possible, those few thousands
would need, not merely now to erect a score or so of
barricades, but to face a predominantly hostile army and
navy armed with engines of modern warfare, with which
a handful of determined men might easily crush the whole
revolutionary force and of which the revolutionaries
themselves could scarcely obtain possession without cap-
turing the national arsenals. Besides this, that handful
of men would have to guarantee the food and control
the transport system of an infinitely complex society,
and, having accomplished all this, they would in almost
all modern societies be dependent upon the benevolent
approval of the states upon which their national trade
depended.

Of all this Marx was ignorant. He had seen France

passing from revolution to revolution, each seeming to
remodel society according to the will of a minority. He
neither realised the already patent, nor the implicit,
obstacles to his ultimate revolution. And so, thanks to
a tempting misinterpretation of the history of France—
and 1793 has been too much for heads less inflamed with
bitterness than his—Marx made that confident false
prophecy which has needlessly obsessed the imagination
of Europe ever since and to which, in the last resort,
he owes so much of his lasting influence.

Such was the new and external force which was to
desiccate and harden the confused and luxurious growths
of the native socialism of France. The French founders
of the International, however, were not disciples of Marx;
in their modest rooms, 44 rue des Gravilliers, they debated, as students, not conspirators, the gradual and
peaceful, the all but imperceptible, transformation of
society by workers' associations : *mutuellistes*, they
called themselves. Cautious to a fault, they were determined not to compromise themselves politically : too
many workmen had been killed already on the barricades
in the interests of the liberal or republican bourgeoisie :
in future they would admit to their society only genuine
manual workers. Jacobins and communists alike con-
temned these modest beginnings : " Imperialist socialism " they called it, affecting to see in the *mutuellistes*
the secret agents of the Empire. In 1867, however, the
International began to make something like a stir. The
successful strike of the Paris bronze-workers of that year
was supported by contributions from the working-men
of London, Manchester, and Birmingham. In November
the French society even demonstrated in the streets, and
in 1868 it was twice proceeded against by the government.
The students had become conspirators. It was in the

same year that the Congress, at Brussels, first committed
itself to State ownership of the means of production.
It is said that by 1870 there were seventy thousand
adherents in Paris and in all France no less than two
hundred thousand.

In April, 1870, the Emperor once again appealed by
plebiscite to France ; the people was invited to approve
the liberal reforms of the Empire since 1860. It accorded
the required approval by 7,358,786 votes against
1,571,939. It is important to examine the details of the
voting a little more closely.[1] In the great towns—Paris,
Lyons, Marseilles, Bordeaux, Toulouse and Saint-
Etienne—the *noes* were in a large majority. And the
strongest opposition, outside the great towns, came from
the South-East and the Valley of the Rhone, in fact from
precisely the districts where there had been socialist
insurrections after the *coup d'état*. Two most significant
conclusions must result from these facts.

First, the Empire had failed to solve the problem
which had confronted it from its creation. Glory and
Order had been the promises of the Napoleonic legend,
and neither had any attraction for that great industrial
population which had grown up *after* the creation of the
legend. Napoleon the third had spent his early years in
developing that revision of the tradition initiated by
Napoleon on St. Helena—a needless revision which, as
we saw, played no part in winning him his throne ; but
he had overlooked the only revision which could have
been of service to him, one which might have added to
the traditional formulæ some hope for the industrial
workers. And so the industrial workers remained where
they had been, excluded ; nor in its nineteen years
had the Empire, in spite of its sumptuous and extensive

[1] For some details see de la Gorce : *Histoire du second Empire*, vi. 114-116.

public works and its partial license of workmen's associations, advanced a jot towards attaching them to itself. The voting on the plebiscite of 1870 is enough to show that the party of the new Revolution was still composed of the same elements, and still implacably hostile.

But the voting has a second and an even greater significance. It made it clearer than it had ever been that the will of the great towns, and particularly of Paris, was completely divergent from that of the country districts of France. Indeed, the results of the voting in Paris were known before those of the rest of France, and the revolutionary parties there had the additional mortification of having the jubilation of their first successes swamped by the overwhelming conservatism of the peasants. And hence directly springs the theory of the Commune, which was an attempt to emancipate the towns from the control of the countryside. The voting on the plebiscites of the Empire underlined for the Revolution the bitter lesson of June, 1848. This time Paris should not be taken unawares by France.

Thus by 1870 the social Revolution which had been overwhelmed by France in 1848, and by Napoleon in 1851, was ready, behind the new theory of the Commune, for another conflict : by itself it could no more hope to overthrow the Empire than by itself it could have overthrown the July monarchy in 1848. But if the Empire should collapse suddenly before disaster from without, abetted perhaps by a general contempt such as that which overthrew the monarchy of July, might it not shoulder out the milder majority of bourgeois republicans and fill the void (as the social revolutionaries had so nearly contrived to fill it in 1848) with its own more violent and Utopian creed ? So the revolutionaries began to hope, and at least it was clear that in spite of the plebiscite the discontent was gathering ominously and needed only now some shock to the weakening fabric of Empire from without. The growth and nature of this widespread discontent belongs rather to the history of the Empire than to the history of the revolutionary idea : irreverence had been contagious since the relaxation of the Press Laws in 1867, taking shape now in the scurrilous witticisms of Rochefort's *La Lanterne*,[1] now in Erckmann and Chatrian's laborious review of the first Empire from the sordid underside of the conscript and the casualty list ; while the insubordinates of the Chamber had grown from the impotent " Five " who faced the serried ranks of government nominees in the muzzled Chamber of 1857 to the famous hundred and sixteen who signed the demand for accelerated reform in 1869. " The Republic," wrote the socialist, Malon, in November, 1869, " is morally proclaimed." And it is not too much to say that from the summer of 1869 the Empire was spiritually dead ; it awaited only the *coup de grâce* to its material

---

[1] Writers who refer to Rochefort confine themselves with curious regularity to de la Gorce's few quotations from him (and these come almost all from Rochefort's first number). But *la Lanterne* can be recommended as the most excellent reading throughout. The following are two good examples of his bitter, allusive manner in its less scurrilous vein :—

" Monday, August 10. Seventy-eight years ago to-day at this very hour the people was plundering the Tuileries. To-day it is exactly the reverse."

And again (he complains of having been accused of "systematic opposition") with some pleasant allusions to the Mexican imbroglio, written in 1868 :

" My opposition is systematic, I admit, but, to be fair, so is the admiration of the *Constitutionnel*.

" As long as so many of our great men systematically pocket 250 to 300,000 francs a year :

" As long as M. Rouher systematically maintains that the Mexican expedition is the great inspiration of the reign (not of Maximilian's reign, of course) ;

" As long in fact as the country seems to me to get on systematically badly, I shall systematically reiterate that it doesn't get on well.

" When Cortez (one of the thousand and one conquerors of Mexico who has subsequently been superseded by brigands) stretched the favourite of Guatimozin on a white-hot grid-iron, he probably complained of the unhappy Aztec's protests at being roasted as ' systematic opposition ' to himself."

structure. The *coup de grâce* was being busily prepared in Berlin.

The end, when it came, came with merciful rapidity. On July 14th, 1870, France declared war on Prussia. On September 2nd the Emperor and 80,000 Frenchmen surrendered to von Moltke at Sedan. On September 3rd the news was known in Paris, and on September 4th the people of Paris proclaimed the Republic. This was the Revolution of 1870. There had been no resistance. No one laid down his life for the Empire.

Once more the Republic had returned, and with it the logical fulfilment of the old Revolution ; and once more it was a Conservative Republic. But, like the Republic of 1848, it had still to survive the assault of the new Revolution.

The Provisional Government formed on September 4th assumed the title of " Government of National Defence." Under General Trochu it remained in Paris through the siege, sending a delegation to Tours to govern the rest of France. On January 28th, 1871, Paris had capitulated; an armistice was signed, imposing on France a general peace on Prussia's conditions in order to obviate in the interests of Paris the probable rigours of a peace made with the capital alone. A National Assembly was to be elected, and the National Assembly would choose between peace and war. This Assembly was elected on February 8th. Its majority was monarchist and in favour of peace, and on February 17th it proceeded to elect Thiers dictator by acclamation ; for Thiers had opposed the later foreign policy of the second Empire and after September 4th had declared for peace rather than the now hopeless war. On February 28th Thiers submitted to the Assembly the terms of the peace he had discussed with Bismarck since February 19th. The Assembly, sitting at Bordeaux, accepted them, although they included the cession of Alsace-Lorraine and the entry of the Prussian army into Paris. Immediately Paris rose.

Throughout the siege of Paris a minority of republicans had not ceased to hope, remembering 1793, the Committee of Public Safety and the *levée en masse*, for a national effort which would even yet save France from the Prussians. To many of them Trochu, governor of Paris, and the chiefs of the National Defence had seemed cowardly, if not treacherous ; the national effort, which they awaited, did not come.

> "This Paris, for which Hoche, Marceau, Kleber would have been neither too young, nor too faithful, nor too pure, had for generals the residue of the Empire and Orleanism. . . . In their pleasant intimacy they made much fun of the defence."

So wrote Lissagaray, apologist and eye-witness of the Commune. And to this cowardice of the defence was added now the undoubted hostility to Paris of the majority of the newly-elected assembly which established itself not at Paris, but at Versailles, abolished the moratorium on rent and other obligations accumulated during the siege, appointed an unpopular commander to the National Guard, and cut off its pay. So France, it seemed, which had conquered Paris and the economic Revolution in the bloody street-fighting of 1848 and had swamped with her apathy the protest of the Parisians and the revolutionaries in the plebiscite of 1870, this France of the "brutal rurals" (the words are Lissagaray's) was once again to betray the country and to betray it this time not only to the possessing classes but to the Prussians ? Paris struck quickly. In February had been formed a "central committee" of the National Guard, which proposed to concern itself not merely with the affairs of the National Guard but with the safety of the Republic. On March 10th this committee refused to surrender the cannon of the National Guard, and on the 18th the troops sent by the Versailles government to retake them were repulsed and the " central committee " established itself at the Hôtel de Ville. France settled down to besiege Paris before the observant Prussians. The Revolution of 1871 had begun.

Eight days later, on March 26th, was elected the Council General of the Commune of Paris—with a large majority for the recent Revolution. The Council General assumed the government of Paris, but the central committee of the National Guard did not dissolve ; and it is this twofold and somewhat indeterminate authority which is known as " the Commune." Necessarily the ingredients of the Commune were heterogeneous. Of the seventy-eight members who sat in the Council General about twenty only could be said to be orthodox Marxians of the International, though there was a tail of vaguer socialists whose intellectual origins were in 1848 ; about twenty more were followers of Blanqui, inevitable products of violence who considered violent revolution a good in itself and aimed at no preciser consummation ; and the rest were Jacobins of the tradition of 1793, without precise economic theories but dreaming patriotically of the Terror and the *levée en masse*. The men who made up the " Commune " were thus of many sorts ; they were not all for the economic Revolution and would have quarrelled unappeasably as to their social policy had they ever been in a position to enforce one. But upon one thing they were in substantial agreement—the principle of the Commune. And the principle of the Commune was the indispensable preliminary to the new Revolution.

As we have seen, the over-preponderance of Paris in France, the tradition that the part is greater than the whole, was much older than the Revolution. For more than one century Paris had absorbed the intellectual life of France as the intellectual life of England could not conceivably be absorbed by London. We have watched Paris making world-history in 1789 while France looked on, passive if expectant. Indeed, the hegemony of Paris was only seriously questioned in the early months of the Convention, and the catastrophe of those who questioned it was rapid and complete. It was not till 1848 that France first met and worsted her own capital. Unluckily the political differences of the strange disputants did not abate under the second Empire : as we have seen, they were already flaring up anew with the plebiscite of 1870. Indeed, with the recent growth of the industrial centres, it becomes more accurate now to speak not so much of the political antagonism between France and Paris as of the social antagonism between the great towns and the country districts. Lissagaray's " brutal rurals " is the bitter cry of the Communard, and in 1871 the proclamation of the Commune in Paris was imitated in Lyons, St. Etienne and Creuzot as well as in Marseilles, Toulouse and Narbonne.

The dispute, although an issue now between great towns and countryside rather than between capital and nation, remained fundamentally unchanged. Was the countryside majority to be dictated to by the urban minorities ?—such was the quarrel still, but its complexion had been altered by the industrial Revolution. It was not now merely a question between an "advanced" politically conscious Paris and an apathetic France : the new industrialism had made a new division in the national life, had given to the town workers a new and bitter

grievance, a distinctive and urgent interest. Beneath its
crude excesses the tragedy of the Commune, and the
theory of the Communards, were in effect no more than
the clear statement for the first time in France—and a
statement the more bitter for its unnaturally long
suppression by the second Empire—of the principal
problem of our day, the problem of the soul of man under
the industrial system. Not that the Commune made any
serious attempt to grapple with economic problems ; it
was too busy fighting : but the bulk of the Communards
had realised that the inevitable preliminary to any
solution of industrial discontents must be some re-
organisation of the political system which could free the
industrial populations of the great towns to work out
their own salvation without being outvoted by rural
majorities ignorant of their peculiar discontents. In
other words, the system of the Commune was to be the
forerunner of the now receding economic Revolution :
1848 had shown that without some such preparation the
economic revolution was foredoomed. And so once more,
as in 1793, Paris was attempting a re-interpretation of
democracy. But this time the dictatorship of the minority
was clearly to pursue the interests of the minority ; it
had no longer the justification of 1793—that its supreme
and only purpose was the salvation of the *patrie en
danger*.

To free Paris, and the great towns, from the countryside—clearly then this was the purpose of the Commune.
At present the government controlled the countryside
and the countryside the towns. There was only one
solution—to reduce to the barest possible minimum the
exaggerated centralisation which endured as the legacy
of the *ancien régime* and the first Napoleon, and to leave
to local bodies not only full powers of self-administration

but the right of social self-development and self-organisation. In other words, France must become a federation of autonomous communes. And this is the meaning of the Communard theory in one at least of its two aspects, and Paris in 1871 was claiming from France that federation which in 1793 had been (through the Girondins) her bitterest charge against France. This federation of self-governing units was at least the *primâ facie* motive of the Communards of Paris ; and in so far Paris might appear the beneficent liberator of France. " Paris," writes Lissagaray of the proclamation of the Commune, " broke the thousand fetters which bound France down to the ground . . . restored the circulation to her paralysed limbs ; said, ' the life of the whole nation exists in each of her smallest organisms ; the unity of the hive, and not that of the barracks.' " Such was the liberator's rôle adopted by Paris at the outset of her adventure and the manifesto of April 19th particularises the " inherent rights " of every Commune. These include vote of the communal budget ; local taxation ; control of local education and police ; choice and control of the magistracy ; and complete individual liberty and rights of public meeting ; control of urban defence and National Guard. With such full powers surely the individual commune might work out its own salvation ?

But the ultimate aim of Paris was in fact something quite other than the independence of all the local units of France, and beneath its superficial appearance of federalism the theory led quite logically, and only by a different path, to the familiar conclusion—the despotism of Paris. For the villages and the smaller towns of France were (and indeed remain) notoriously incompetent to transact the most everyday local business. France has

never had a training in local self-government, and the
first two years of the Revolution of 1789, as we have
seen, had been by themselves sufficient to demonstrate
the absurdity of the complete local autonomy which had
made of France a mere *poussière tourbillonnante*. To include the countryside of France in such a federation of
independent units could only have meant its subordina-
tion to the great cities, and primarily to Paris, instead
of to the centralised government. And this is the second
and the truer aspect of the theory of the Commune.
Beneath their seductive talk of the " inherent rights "
of every commune this was, no doubt, or became as
circumstances forced its necessity upon them, the
objective of the majority of Communards : the " brutal
rurals " were once more to be relegated to their proper
place. Lissagaray's comment upon the manifesto of
April 19th is significant of the real meaning of the
movement.

" According to this text, every locality was to shut
itself up within its autonomy. But what to expect of
autonomy in Lower Brittany, in nine-tenths of the
French communes . . . ? No ! Thousands of mutes
and blind are not fitted to conclude a social pact.
Weak, unorganised, bound by a thousand trammels,
*the people of the country can only be saved by the towns,
and the people of the towns guided by Paris.*"
The comment represents what was increasingly the
dominant motive of the Communards, and in any case
must have been the inevitable consequence of the application of their theory—the revived despotism of Paris.

Such is the essential import of the tumultuous gesture
which we call the Commune ; for its theory was infinitely
more significant than its practice. Indeed its practical
achievements are negligible : for it spent its time fighting

and had little time for legislation, and it suffered moreover from the poor quality of the members elected to the
Council, violent talkers rather than men of experience.
Of the ten " commissions " into which the Council
divided itself the Commission of Labour and Exchange
is the most important, if only because it was the Commission of Labour and Exchange which attempted some
rudimentary socialist legislation. The suppression of
pawnshops, the abolition of fining by stoppage of wages
by employers, and of night work among bakers, the
return of deserted workshops to co-operative societies of
workmen, and an elementary labour exchange were all
projected or attempted, and the Commission commenced
an investigation into the system by which government
contracts went to the lowest tender, usually, as it believed,
made possible by reducing not profits but wages. There
is nothing very revolutionary about this, and the Commission of Labour and Exchange was practically the only
commission which achieved any legislation at all : of the
rest the Commissions of War, Public Safety, the Exterior,
Education, and Justice varied only between total and
all but total futility ; that of the municipal services
functioned normally by normal methods and only that
of Finance improvised with genuine ability. The Commune was revolutionary not because of what it did but
because of what it claimed.

For two months the Revolution of Paris maintained
itself desperately against its besiegers, beneath the
cynical observation of the Prussians who held the ring
in the interests of Thiers. On the whole during these
months the Commune was surprisingly guiltless of excess.
But by May 21st the army of Versailles had forced its
way into Paris and there followed a hideous week of
bloodshed in the streets, during which the Communards

in the desperation of defeat shot a number of their
hostages and set fire to the districts captured by the
Versailles troops. By the 28th all was over : guns,
cartridge boxes and uniforms littered the gutters of the
poorer quarters, while in the doorways sat stony-eyed
women waiting chin on hand for the men who would not
come back : and elsewhere more elegant Parisiennes
could be seen trilling with excited laughter as they raised
the covering with the tip of their parasols and peered at
the faces of the dead. The vengeance of the party of
Order was comprehensive and very dreadful, more
dreadful than the vengeance of the Revolution had ever
been, even in 1793 ; the shooting of men, women and
children in hundreds and without trial was a massacre,
not an execution, and not a few of the victims were
buried before they were dead. The details of the savagery
read strangely like those of the atrocities reported of the
Germans in Belgium in 1914. Trials, where they took
place, were travesties as horrible as those of 1793. A
certain Moilin was condemned, as his judges informed
him, " not that he had committed any act that merited
death, but because he was a chief of the socialist party,
one of those men of whom a prudent and wise government must rid itself when it finds a legitimate occasion."

All over Paris huge piles of corpses encumbered the
streets and poisoned the air. The cemeteries of Paris
could not receive a tithe of the butchered. Enormous
ditches at Père Lachaise, Montmartre and Mont-Parnasse
and the trenches of the first siege at Charonne and elsewhere absorbed the unhonoured corpses, while women,
widows and mothers, peered hopelessly among them for
the dead that had been theirs. When the task of burial
became too onerous the corpses were burnt in the open
air. It seems probable that 20,000 were killed during the

few weeks immediately following the victory. The figure is unparalleled ; in modern European history almost unimaginable. And the martyrdom of the prisoners was more dreadful than that of the executed : there were probably between 40,000 and 50,000 of them ;[1] and among them more than a thousand women and seventy children under fourteen ; and the barbarity of their treatment can be matched only in the East ; one must look to the Black Hole of Calcutta or to some of the Armenian massacres for an approach to the brutal savageries of the conquerors. Twenty-two courts-martial sat until 1876, trying the prisoners of the Commune. Perhaps of their sentences execution was to be dreaded less than the death in life of transportation to the Antipodes.

The cruelties of which man is capable are a perpetual marvel : none the less nothing in history, not even the Terror, prepares one for the fate met by Frenchmen at the hands of Frenchmen in 1871, the age of Gladstone, the year in which Lowe was creating a sensation in England by proposing the taxation of lucifer matches. It was a party of women, dying of thirst, who were forced by their fellow countrymen to drink from a pond red with the blood of their own people. It was by their own countrymen that prisoners were piled for twenty-four hours, and longer, at a time in stifling cattle-waggons without ventilation or drink or room to stir, and it was their own countrymen who, when the cries from the waggons grew too loud, fired at random into the mass of humanity within. Such was the vengeance of the possessing classes upon the dispossessed, of the old

---

[1] See Lissagaray on the massacres, and the inferno of the prisoners. Lissagaray of course is a partisan, but his evidence is convincing. General Appert, at the head of military justice, admitted 17,000 victims and 38,568 prisoners.

Revolution upon the new, of the provinces upon Paris ; its details do not, like those of the Terror, find their way into history, but they repay some examination, most dreadful among all the dreadful annals of Revolution.

The new Revolution had lost its leaders with a great part, and that the most active, of its rank and file. Once more it passes from sight ; and when it reappears— beyond the range of our present purpose—it reappears in the new guise of syndicalism, still theoretic rather than practical, touched still, as the *Reflexions sur la violence* of Sorel, its philosopher, bears witness, with something of the tradition of the terrorist and the idealogue. The dreadful story of 1871 is the last act of the drama of which we have been spectators. Once more the Revolution of 1789 affirms itself as the permanent settlement of France against the challenge of the new Revolution. And here too, at least for France and England, the history of violent revolution seems to end. It is possible that a great military defeat, as with Germany in 1918, a great famine or pestilence, may yet bring about a social upheaval. Apparently, too, mankind does not outgrow violence ; none the less and in spite of recent happenings in Ireland or Italy all the evidence seems to show that an organised Revolution to change the constitution of society is not likely to occur and if it occurs cannot succeed. Such changes can be effected only by majorities, and majorities have usually other means of enforcing their desires. I say "usually" : for it is always conceivable that the majority of a nation might desire a change in the economic struc- ture of society which a small, economically powerful minority was able to prevent. In which event we should see once more the Revolution of a majority.

CHAPTER IX

CONCLUSION

THERE are then two French Revolutions. The first—which had spent both its aggressive and its constructive force by 1814, but which includes the conservative rising of 1830 and subsists thereafter as a conservative force—achieved a gigantic result, nothing less than the permanent remaking of France ; and it achieved it probably with the infliction of no more suffering than was caused by the government's suppression of the brief revolt of the Communards in 1871. The second Revolution—which was crushed in 1848 and again in 1871—at great cost achieved no positive results at all. What does this acute contrast teach us as to the nature of Revolutions ?

And, first, it is worth while to notice that the opinions popularly held and the conclusions popularly drawn in England concerning the two Revolutions are on the whole the precise contrary to the truth. The " average, unphilosophic man " supposes that the first, the great, Revolution accomplished little or nothing at a vast expense of blood and misery. And the explanation of his error is not difficult. It is due in the first place to a natural misunderstanding of the rôle of the first Bonaparte. To the unreflecting spectator the Revolution, in accepting a Cæsar, may excusably appear to have been

174

unconditionally surrendering, where in truth, as we have
seen, it was but welcoming for its own purposes a great
servant who would pursue its own ends. The Empire,
as we have seen, was nothing more nor less than the final
stage of the Revolution. And, secondly, the popular
misjudgment is due to the literary, often propagandist,
representation of the Terror. For the Terror has long
since passed from the domain of history to that of literature. The romantic possibilities for a certain type of
fiction-maker of the drama of aristocrat and sansculotte
are too great : and, needless to say, the sansculotte is
not its hero. How many moving (and imaginative) pic-
tures are there not of human tragedy under the first
Terror ? Is there one of human tragedy under the
Terror of 1871 ?

These two misconceptions of Bonaparte and of the
Terror, I think, largely explain the popular misconceptions of the great Revolution. And yet, in spite of this
complete miscalculation of its success and cost the
" average, unphilosophic man " does none the less suppose that French history has somehow proved the terrible
ease with which Revolutions may be made and may
succeed. This is indeed the second great popular error
of which I spoke. Its explanation is not difficult. All the
three French Revolutions of the nineteenth century, 1830,
1848, and 1870—and we might count them five if we
chose to include in our reckoning the events of 1814 and
1815—involved the overthrow of a reigning house, while
the fourth Revolution, that of 1871, seen at a distance,
appeared little more than the aftermath of 1870. Now
to English eyes nothing appears more catastrophic than
the expulsion of a sovereign dynasty, and it is easy to
understand how the history of France in the nineteenth
century came to be thought of as an apotheosis of facile

and successful revolution-making. Even to-day, indeed, this misjudgment contributes to the strange disquietude revived by the successful Russian Revolution in western countries where conditions do not remotely resemble those of Russia. We have thus the curious position that by the unreflecting the history of France is wrongly supposed to prove the continued possibility of successful Revolution and that this proof is found not in the Revolution which did in fact succeed but in those which in fact did not.

Such then, in parenthesis, are the two erroneous but popular opinions concerning the French Revolutions. What lesson are we ourselves to draw ? And here we must return to our contrast between the success of the first, and the failure of the second, revolutionary movement. What essential difference in character or circumstances accounts for their difference in result ? And in answering this question we ought to come to some conclusion as to the possibilities of Revolution in other countries.

In the first place the Revolution of 1789 was permanently successful because it was *national*, whereas the attempts at economic Revolution in 1848 and 1871 were the efforts of a small minority. It is perfectly true that during a phase of the first Revolution, for more than two years, let us say, from 1792 to 1794, France was ruled against its inclination by a minority, and that this prolonged and successful minority-rule was possible in the France of 1792 with its undeveloped communications and was not possible in the more highly organised France of 1848 or 1871, with its more elaborate system of communications. But although lack of communications and political apathy made minority rule possible for a while in 1792, nothing but the assent of the great majority of the nation could have made the results achieved by the Revolution permanent. The dictatorship of a minority was not possible at all in 1848, still less in 1871 : it was ónly possible for a limited period even in 1792, and then principally because of the imminent peril of conquest by foreign invaders : when that peril had receded, the dictatorship of the minority collapsed.

The first Revolution was successful, that is to say, it effected great and permanent changes, because such changes were desired by the majority of the nation. Before 1789 the great majority of the nation—broadly speaking, the whole of the middle classes and the peasants —desired either the re-organisation of government or the destruction of feudalism (the two great ends of which we have spoken as Order and Equality) or both. By 1814 these two purposes had been achieved—the middle classes had received strong and efficient government and the career open to talent, and as for the peasants, they had been liberated from the overwhelming burden of feudalism and had got possession of the land. The nation as a whole thankfully assented to these profound modifications of the structure of national life. It was, necessarily, the activity of a minority which accomplished them, but they could have been accomplished only with difficulty, and could not have endured at all, without the consent of the vast majority of the people of France. This is the one ultimate reason why the first Revolution was successful. And this great fact too, the assent of France, stultifies the partial but too common picture of the Revolution which concentrates all attention upon the cruelties of the Terror or the obscure undercurrents of revolutionary plotting. The first Revolution was the work of France ; that is at once its justification and the cause of its success.

Another cause of that success—or it may be considered another aspect of the same cause—which likewise differentiates the first Revolution from the second is that, taking the Revolution as a whole, it was a movement which had grown slowly through many years. The Revolution, as I have shown, was in being long before 1789. Its " outbreak " in that year was not due to the fallible decision of a handful of conspirators but to the inscrutable provision in circumstances of an outlet for explosion, which, had circumstances fallen otherwise, might have come sooner or later, but in any event must have come.

It was otherwise with the second Revolution—of 1848 and 1871, the economic Revolution (for both, as I have said, were social Revolutions). Very strikingly this was the Revolution of a minority, a minority even of Paris. France, with its highly centralised government, its concentration of political and intellectual life in the capital, and its tradition of provincial apathy, was the most susceptible of highly organised states to a minority Revolution. But even in France neither rising was able to do more than maintain itself precariously for a few weeks. How much less could it have effected any lasting modification of the social structure ! The accident that three times a reigning dynasty fell unresisting was not strictly the work of the revolutionaries. Twice the economic Revolution did its best to seize power in order to remodel society, and twice it failed. Some of the reasons why in a highly organised society the Revolution of a minority must always fail I have enumerated in discussing the prophecy of Marx. These reasons are implicit in modern society, and may be studied there in detail. Some of them have become apparent in the course of our sketch ; but in this matter of the possibility of

minority Revolutions the clearest lesson taught by it is
to be learnt from the wider fact that for a highly civilised
society France in the nineteenth century offered unex-
ampled opportunities for a successful minority Revolution and yet always the minority Revolution failed.
What would be the prospects of success in a modern
state of Revolution by a *majority* is another and a deeper
problem, and I express no opinion upon it here.

In presenting in bare outline the succeeding phases of
the revolutionary idea I have been at no pains to pass
moral judgments upon it. And yet incidentally I have
drawn attention to the possibility of wrong judgments.
The most fertile source of misjudgment, as we saw, is the
unphilosophic view which understands by the French
Revolution the history of France during the years over
which the Revolution extends. It is easy enough with
such presumptions to present the Revolution as culpable
out of all semblance to truth. The Terror, with such
presumptions, becomes a vast crime (though even so no
vaster than that of 1871). But not more than half the
responsibility for the Terror belongs to the true Revolution, to the national will, that is, for certain changes and
the effort to achieve them. Again, I have noticed here
and there a few of the inevitable ineptitudes of any
attempt to present the Revolution, in all its phases, as
the blind struggle of dupes impelled all unknowing by a
hidden but permanent conspiracy to " destroy civilisation " : but such a view, with the estimate it implies
of ordinary humanity, and its blindness to the overwhelming debt of the civilisation of Europe to-day to
this very Revolution, needs in truth no detailed exposure.
Any unprejudiced account of the origins of the revolutionary idea must be its refutation.

Lastly it is worth while to notice that the Revolutions

of the nineteenth century in the other countries of
Europe were not of the same kind as those of France,
although particularly in 1848 they followed their French
predecessor with curious celerity, and although at the
time many French revolutionaries mistook them for
imitations. The first French Revolution has had an
altogether incalculable effect upon political thought and
practice all over Europe, and far more effect there than
it has ever produced in England. It was unique in that
it was not only national but international : the deputies
to the Constituent Assembly felt themselves representatives not of France only but mankind. And yet, although
the French Revolution has in varying degrees become
part of every civilised state, there has been no European
Revolution of the same nature. It was not needed. Some
of the work done in France by the Revolution was done
upon the continent of Europe by the Napoleonic armies
of occupation or by the Napoleonic Empire which
destroyed the *ancien régime* far beyond the boundaries
of France. The rest was accomplished at other times and
in other ways or has not yet been accomplished at all.
As for the second, the economic Revolution, the objects
at which it aimed are pursued in all European countries
but there has been no genuine attempt at a violent
economic Revolution outside France.[1] Outside France
the Revolutions of the nineteenth century were either
merely liberal, like that of Spain in 1820, or merely
nationalist, like those of Greece in 1821 or Lombardy in
1848, or both together like those in Germany in 1848.
Socialist thought in England and Germany did not lag
behind that of France, but in France Socialism found
both the revolutionary temperament and two Revolutions ready made for its exploitation. And hence the

[1] In this connection Russia is not a European country.

unique character of French history. Socialist thought
has followed in other countries very much the lines
which it followed in France, and the mistake has been
too commonly made of supposing that other countries
must necessarily share also the revolutionary history
which for a while accompanied it in France. There will
be Revolutions again only if the conditions of the France
of 1789 are reproduced. Only, that is to say, if the
majority of a nation needs and desires a change and a
privileged minority is able to prevent that change from
being brought about by constitutional or peaceful
methods.

SHORT LIST OF BOOKS

A.—For 1789-1799.

GENERAL

*DE TOCQUEVILLE	. *L'ancien régime et la Révolution.*
*A. AULARD .	. *Histoire politique de la Révolution française.*
*L. MADELIN .	. *La Révolution française.*
LORD ACTON .	. Lectures on the French Revolution.
SOREL . .	. *L'Europe et la Révolution française.*
*BOURGEOIS .	. *Manuel historique de politique étrangère,* Vol. 2.
MORSE-STEPHENS	. History of the French Revolution.

CHAPTER I.

LOWELL . .	. France on the eve of the Revolution.
A. AULARD .	. *La Révolution française et le régime féodal.*
ARTHUR YOUNG	. Travels in France.
TAINE . .	. *Origines de la France contemporaine,* Vol. I.
J. B. BURY .	. The Idea of Progress.
MME. DE STAËL	. *Considérations.*
BURKE . .	. Reflections on the French Revolution.
ROUSSEAU .	. *Du Contrat Social.*

CHAPTER II.

*MIRABEAU .	. *Correspondance avec le Comte de la Marck.*
WILLERT .	. Life of Mirabeau.
J. B. BURY .	. *Op. cit.*
THIÉBAULT .	. *Mémoires.*
A. AULARD .	. *Op. cit.*
MORSE-STEPHENS	. Orators of the French Revolution.
WICKHAM LEGG	. Select Documents of the French Revolution.
SCHMIDT .	. *Tableaux de la Révolution française.*
CARLYLE .	. French Revolution (*ed.* C. R. L. Fletcher).
MRS. N. H. WEBSTER	The French Revolution : A Study in Democracy.

182

CHAPTER III.

SCHMIDT . . *Op. cit.*
MORSE-STEPHENS . Orators of the French Revolution.
*COCHIN . . . *La crise de l'histoire révolutionnaire.*
THIÉBAULT . . *Op. cit.*
BUZOT . . . *Mémoires.*
LEVASSEUR DE LA
   SARTHE . *Mémoires.*
LANDAU-ALDANOV *Deux révolutions.*
R. W. POSTGATE . Revolution from 1789 to 1908.
G. D. H. COLE . Social Theory.
ROBESPIERRE . *Œuvres.*
LENÔTRE . . *Les massacres de septembre.*
MRS. N. H. WEBSTER *Op. cit.*
L. MADELIN . . *Danton.*
LAMARTINE . . *Histoire des Girondins.*
JOHN MOORE . Journal during a residence in France (1793).
TAINE . . *Origines de la France contemporaine.*
MME. ROLAND . *Mémoires.*
ANATOLE FRANCE *Les dieux ont soif.*
GUÉNIN AND
   NOUAILLAC . *L'ancien régime et la révolution.*
DUMOURIEZ . *Mémoires.*

CHAPTER IV.

SCHMIDT . . *Op. cit.*
MRS. H. N. WEBSTER *Op. cit.*
MRS. H. N. WEBSTER World Revolution : The Plot against
   Civilisation.
*VANDAL . . . *L'avènement de Bonaparte.* Vol. 2.
*H. A. L. FISHER . Bonapartism.
HOLLAND ROSE . Napoleon I.
SEELEY . . . Short History of Napoleon I.
MME. DE STAËL . *Considérations.*
BODLEY . . . Modern France.
AULARD . . . *La révolution française et le régime féodal.*
LECARPENTIER . *Les biens nationaux.*
LICHTENBERGER . *Le socialisme et la révolution.*
BAILLEUL . . *Examen des considérations de Mme. de Staël.*
DE GONCOURT . *La Société sous le Directoire.*

B.—For 1814-1871.

GENERAL.

*BOURGEOIS . . Modern France.
*SEIGNOBOS . . *Histoire de l'Europe contemporaine.*

CHAPTER V.

BONALD . . .	*Pensées.*
BONALD . . .	*Mélanges littéraires politiques et philosophiques*
CHATEAUBRIAND .	*Œuvres* (esp. *Mélanges politiques*).
DE MAISTRE . .	*du Pape.*
*LOUIS BLANC .	*Histoire de dix ans.*
GUIZOT . . .	*Mémoires.*

CHAPTER VI.

THUREAU-DANGIN	*Histoire de la Monarchie de Juillet.*
BOURGEOIS . .	*Manuel historique de politique étrangère.*
VICTOR HUGO .	*Les Misérables.*
*DE TOCQUEVILLE	*Souvenirs.*
NASSAU SENIOR .	Conversations with distinguished persons under the Second Empire.
CHATEAUBRIAND .	*Œuvres.*
M. HOVELL . .	The Chartist Movement.
S. AND B. WEBB .	A History of Trade Unionism.
MRS. WEBSTER .	World Revolution : The Plot against Civilisation.
FOURIER . .	(See works quoted above, p. 119).
PROUDHON . .	*Mémoire sur la propriété.*
LAMARTINE . .	*Histoire de la Révolution de* 1848.
CABET . . .	*Voyage en Icarie.*
JANET . . .	*Saint-Simon et le Saint-Simonisme.*
*SAINT-SIMON .	*Œuvres* (esp. vols. XX-XXII).
*LOUIS BLANC .	*L'organisation du travail.*

Analyse de la doctrine de Babœuf, 1795.

CHAPTER VII.

*DE TOCQUEVILLE	*Op. cit.*
LAMARTINE . .	*Op. cit.*
LOUIS BLANC .	*Histoire de la Révolution.*
P. DE LA GORCE .	*Histoire de la Révolution.*
THOMAS . . .	*Histoire des Ateliers Nationaux.*
MRS. WEBSTER .	*Op. cit.*
HECKTHORN . .	Secret Societies.
BARROT . .	*Mémoires.*
F. A. SIMPSON .	The Rise of Louis Napoleon.
NAPOLEON III .	*Des idées Napoléoniennes.*
P. GUEDALLA .	The Second Empire.
*H. A. L. FISHER .	*Op. cit.*

CHAPTER VIII.

DE LA GORCE . *Histoire du seconde Empire.*
*H. A. L. FISHER . *Op. cit.*
P. GUEDALLA . *Op. cit.*
BERTRAND RUSSELL Roads to Freedom
NASSAU SENIOR . *Op. cit.*
LANO . . . *Cour de Napoleon III.*
KARL MARX . . Communist Manifesto.
KARL MARX . . Capital.
H. J. LASKI . . Karl Marx.
MRS. N. H. WEBSTER *Op. cit.*
*LOWES-DICKINSON Revolution and reaction in modern France.
SOREL . . . *Reflexions sur la violence.*
ERCKMANN-
CHATRIAN . . *Histoire d'un conscrit de* 1813.
ROCHEFORT . . *La Lanterne.*
*LISSAGARAY . . *Histoire de la Commune.*
THIERS . . . *Notes et Souvenirs.*
F. A. SIMPSON . Louis Napoleon and the Recovery of France (1848-1856).

CHRONOLOGICAL TABLE

1751-1765. The Encyclopædia.

1762. Rousseau's *Contrat Social*.

1767. Mercier de la Riviere's *L'ordre naturel et essentiel des sociétés politiques*.

1774. Accession of Louis XVI.
   Turgot *contrôleur général.*

1776 Necker *contrôleur général*

1781. Necker dismissed.

1787. First Meeting of the Notables.
   The struggle with the Parlements.

1788. Necker recalled. States General summoned.
   Nov. Second Meeting of Notables.

1789. May 5. Meeting of the States General.
   June. The States General become the National Constituent Assembly.
   July 14. Taking of the Bastille.
   Aug. 4. The Constituent Assembly begins to vote the destruction of Feudalism.
   Declaration of rights.
   Oct. 5. March of the women to Versailles.
   Nov. 7. "*Motion Lanjuinais*."

1790. Feb. The Constituent Assembly concludes its discussion of the new Constitution known as the Constitution of 1791
   May. Mirabeau's letters to the Court begin.
   May 22. "France renounces the idea of conquest."
   July 12. The Constituent Assembly passes the "Civil Constitution of the Clergy."

1791. April 2. Death of Mirabeau.
   Sept.14. The Constitution of 1791 accepted by the King.
   Oct. 1. Meeting of the Legislative Assembly.
   Nov. 29. The Assembly "threatens in the jargon of pacifism."

1792. April 20. War declared on Austria.
   June 18. The Assembly abolishes the *droits casuels*.
   July 25. Brunswick's Manifesto.
   July 29. Prussia declares war.
   Aug. 9-10. Birth of the Revolutionary Commune.

1792. Aug. 10. Invasion of the Tuileries.
             Suspension of the King.
      Aug. 25. The Assembly abolishes all feudal dues whatever
             without indemnity, unless their original titles can
             be produced.
      Sept. 2-6. September massacres.
      Sept. 20. Battle of Valmy.
      Sept. 20. First meeting of the Convention.
      Sept. 21. Abolition of royalty.
      Nov. 6. Battle of Jemmappes.
1793. Jan. 21. Execution of the King.
      Feb. 1. France declares war on England.
      March 9. Decree authorising *représentants en mission*.
      March 10. Institution of the Revolutionary Tribunal.
      April 3. Treachery of Dumouriez.
      April 6. Election of the Committee of Public Safety.
      June 2. Proscription of the Girondins.
      July 17. Suppression of all remaining feudal dues.
1794. March 29. Execution of Hébert.
      April 3. Execution of Danton.
      July 28. Execution of Robespierre.
1795. Nov. 3. Inauguration of the Directory.
1796. Bonaparte in Italy.
      Arrest and execution of Babœuf.
1799. Nov. 10. Coup d'état of Brumaire. Bonaparte first consul.
1804. Dec. 2. Coronation of Napoleon as Emperor.
1814. April 11. First abdication of Napoleon.
      June.   The Bourbon charter.
1815. March 13-June 22.   The Hundred Days of Napoleon's return.
      April 22. The *acte additionel*.
      August.   Election of the *chambre introuvable*.
1816. Sept.   The King dissolves the *chambre introuvable*.
      Nov.   New chamber with majority for the revolutionary
             settlement.
1817. Feb.   New electoral law.
1818. Dec.   Resignation of Richelieu.
1820. Saint-Simon's *L'Organisateur*.
      Feb. 13. Murder of Duc de Berri.
      Richelieu in power again.
      April.   New electoral law.
1821. Saint-Simon's *Chatécisme industriel*.
1822. March 18. Press law.
      Nov.   Chateaubriand at the Congress of Verona.
1823. French Intervention in Spain in the interests of absolutism.
1824. Saint-Simon's *Nouveau Christianisme*.
1825. Compensation to the émigrés.
      Death of Saint-Simon.

1826. Law of sacrilege.
1827. Nov.   Feudalist party defeated at the elections.
1828. Jan.   Ministry of Martignac.
       Buonarotti's *Histoire de la conspiration de Babœuf.*
1829. April.   Dismissal of Martignac.
       Fourier's *Nouveau monde industriel.*
1830. July 26. The Four Ordinances.
       July 27. Insurrection.
       Aug. 7. Louis Philippe proclaimed King.
1840. Proudhon's *Mémoire sur la Propriété.*
       Cabet's *Voyage en Icarie.*
       Leroux' *de l'Humanité.*
       Foundation of *L'Atelier.*
       Louis Blanc's *L'Organisation du travail* and *L'histoire de dix
              ans.*
1848 Marx' *Communist Manifesto.*
       Feb. 22, 23. Revolution : first phase.
       Feb. 24-26. Second phase.
       Feb. 27-June 26. Third phase.
       May 4. Meeting of the Constituent Assembly.
       June 24-26. Street fighting.
       December. Louis Napoleon elected President.
1851. Dec. 2. Coup d'état.
1852. Dec. 10. The Second Empire.
1856. Congress of Paris.
1864. The International Association of Workers.
1867. Maximilian shot. End of the Mexican adventure.
1868. Congress of the International at Brussels adopts State owner-
              ship of the means of production.
       Strike of Paris bronze workers.
1869. The Liberal Empire.
1870. April.   Plebiscite.
       July 14. France declares war on Prussia.
       Sept. 2. Sedan.
       Sept. 4. Proclamation of the Republic.
1871. Jan. 28. Capitulation of Paris.
       Feb. 8. Election of National Assembly.
       Feb. 17. Election of Thiers as dictator.
       March 10. Central Committee of National Guard refuses to
              surrender its cannon.
       March 18. Insurrection of the Commune.
       March 26. Election of the Conseil Général of the Commune.
       May 21-28. Street fighting.
       Suppression of the Commune.

INDEX

Saint-Simon, 118, 119, 120, 121,
  122-126, 128
Sedan, 151
Sorel, 157, 173
Sue, Eugène, 112

Thierry, 93
Thiers, 134, 136, 163, 170
Thureau-Dangin, 118, 120, 122,
  128, 129
Trochu, 163, 164
Turgot, 10, 15, 17, 29, 65

Valmy, 73, 74, 91
Villèle, 103, 105, 114
Voltaire, 17, 90
Von Moltke, 163

Webster, Mrs. N. H., 59, 71, 77,
  117, 118, 122, 136
Weishaupt, 119
Wells, H. G., 124

Young, Arthur, 21